WORLD IN CONFLICT

NORTHERN IRELAND

TROUBLED LAND

NORTHERN IRELAND
TROUBLED LAND

by Eric Black

Lerner Publications Company / Minneapolis

13003

Lerner Publications Company
A division of Lerner Publishing Group
241 First Avenue North
Minneapolis, MN 55401 U.S.A.

Website address: www.lernerbooks.com

All maps by Philip Schwartzberg, Meridian Mapping, Minneapolis.
Cover photo © Bruce Haley
Table of Contents photos (from top to bottom) by Northern Ireland
Tourist Board; © Pacemaker Press International Ltd.; Independent
Picture Service; Express News/Archive Photos; Children's Friendship
Project of Northern Ireland, Inc.

Series Consultant: Andrew Bell-Fialkoff
Editorial Director: Mary M. Rodgers
Editor: Cynthia Harris
Designer: Michael Tacheny
Photo Researcher: Gina Germ

LIBRARY OF CONGRESS CATALOGING-IN-PUBLICATION DATA

Black, Eric.
    Northern Ireland : troubled land / by Eric Black.
       p.   cm. — (World in conflict)
    Includes bibliographical references and index.
    Summary: Examines the history of the ethnic conflict in Northern
Ireland, including current issues.
    ISBN 0–8225–3552–1 (lib. bdg. : alk. paper)
    1. Northern Ireland—History—1969–1994—Juvenile literature.
2. Northern Ireland—History—1994– —Juvenile literature.
3. Political violence—Northern Ireland—Juvenile literature.
[1. Northern Ireland—History—1969–1994. 2. Northern Ireland—
History—1994–   ] I. Title. II. Series
DA990.U46B47   1998   96–43639
941.6—dc20
Manufactured in the United States of America
2 3 4 5 6 7 – JR – 05 04 03 02 01 00

CONTENTS

ABOUT THIS SERIES

Government firepower kills 25 protesters . . . Thousands of refugees flee the country . . . Rebels attack capital . . . Racism and rage flare . . . Fighting breaks out . . . Peace talks stall . . . Bombing toll rises to 52 . . . Slaughter has cost up to 50,000 lives.

Conflicts between people occur across the globe, and we hear about some of the more spectacular and horrific episodes in the news. But since most fighting doesn't directly affect us, we often choose to ignore it. And even if we do take the time to learn about these conflicts—from newspapers, magazines, television news, or radio—we're often left with just a snapshot of the conflict instead of the whole reel of film.

Most news accounts don't tell you the whole story about a conflict, focusing instead on the attention-grabbing events that make the headlines. In addition, news sources may have a preconceived idea about who is right and who is wrong in a conflict. The stories that result often portray one side as the "bad guys" and the other as the "good guys."

The *World in Conflict* series approaches each conflict with the idea that wars and political disputes aren't simply about bullies and victims. Conflicts are complex problems that can often be traced back hundreds of years. The people fighting one another have complicated reasons for doing so. Fighting erupts between groups divided by ethnicity, religion, and nationalism. These groups fight over power, money, territory, control. Sometimes people who just want to go about their own business get caught up in a conflict just because they're there.

These books examine major conflicts around the world, some of which are very bloody and others that haven't involved a lot of violence. They portray the people involved in and affected by conflicts. They describe how each conflict got started, how it developed, and where it stands. The books also outline some of the ways people have tried to end the conflicts. By reading the stories behind the headlines, you will learn some reasons why people hate and fight one another and, in addition, why some people struggle so hard to end conflicts.

WORDS YOU NEED TO KNOW

discrimination: The less favorable, prejudicial treatment received by someone because he or she fits into a category that some people, within or outside of the society, hold in low esteem. Examples of categories upon which discrimination may be based include ethnicity, gender, and age.

emancipation: The return of freedom—political or physical—after being under the power and strict control of another person or group.

ethnicity: A combination of cultural markers that bind a people into a distinctive, permanent group. These markers may include—but are not limited to—race, nationality, tribe, religion, language, customs, and historical origins.

guerrilla tactic: A method of fighting that is radical, aggressive, or unconventional. Guerrilla tactics are often used by rebel fighters who are not associated with an internationally recognized government security force.

nationality: A national character. A group of people who because they share race, language, tradition, and origin can be distinguished from other populations. This group may make up or is capable of forming a nation-state.

paramilitary: A supplementary fighting force. Often, but not always, this term is used to describe underground, illegal groups. Sometimes an illegal paramilitary group may support, through the use of violence, the current government and its policies. The aim of other paramilitary groups is the overthrow of the government.

propaganda: Ideas, rumor, or information spread to influence people's opinion. The intent of propaganda may be either to injure or to promote an institution, a cause, or a people.

province: An administrative district.

secede: To formally withdraw membership from a political unit, such as a nation, or from an organization, such as the United Nations. The seceding group usually desires increased independence or autonomy.

sovereignty: Power over a region. In some cases, an outside political entity holds the power; in others, a region has its own independent political control.

FOREWORD

by Andrew Bell-Fialkoff

Conflicts between various groups are as old as time. Peoples and tribes around the world have fought one another for thousands of years. In fact our history is in great part a succession of wars—between the Greeks and the Persians, the English and the French, the Russians and the Poles, and many others. Not only do states or ethnic groups fight one another, so do followers of different religions—Catholics and Protestants in Northern Ireland, Christians and Muslims in Bosnia, and Buddhists and Hindus in Sri Lanka. Often ethnicity, language, and religion—some of the main distinguishing elements of culture—reinforce one another in characterizing a particular group. For instance, the vast majority of Greeks are Orthodox Christian and speak Greek; most Italians are Roman Catholic and speak Italian. Elsewhere, one cultural aspect predominates. Serbs and Croats speak dialects of the same language but remain separate from one another because most Croats are Catholics and most Serbs are Orthodox Christians. To those two groups, religion is more important than language in defining culture.

We have witnessed an increasing number of conflicts in modern times—why? Three reasons stand out. One is that large empires—such as Austria-Hungary, Ottoman Turkey, several colonial empires with vast holdings in Asia, Africa, and America, and, most recently, the Soviet Union—have collapsed. A look at world maps from 1900, 1950, and 1998 reveals an ever-increasing number of small and medium-sized states. While empires existed, their rulers suppressed many ethnic and religious conflicts. Empires imposed order, and local resentments were mostly directed at the central authority. Inside the borders of empires, populations were multiethnic and often highly mixed. When the empires fell apart, world leaders found it impossible to establish political frontiers that coincided with ethnic boundaries. Different groups often claimed territories inhabited by others. The nations created on the lands of a toppled empire were saddled with acute border and ethnic problems from their very beginnings.

The second reason for more conflicts in modern times stems from the twin ideals of freedom and equality. In the United States, we usually think of freedom as "individual freedom." If we all have equal rights, we are free. But if you are a member of a minority group and feel that you are being discriminated against, your group's rights and freedoms are also important to you. In fact, if you don't have your "group freedom," you don't have full individual freedom either.

After World War I (1914–1918), the allied western nations, under the guidance of U.S. president Woodrow Wilson, tried to satisfy group rights by promoting minority rights. The spread of frantic nationalism in the 1930s, especially among disaffected ethnic minorities, and the catastrophe of World War II (1939–1945) led to a fundamental

NORTHERN IRELAND *Troubled Land*

reassessment of the Wilsonian philosophy. After 1945 group rights were downplayed on the assumption that guaranteeing individual rights would be sufficient. In later decades, the collapse of multiethnic nations like Czechoslovakia, Yugoslavia, and the Soviet Union—coupled with the spread of nationalism in those regions—came as a shock to world leaders. People want democracy and individual rights, but they want their group rights, too. In practice, this means more conflicts and a cycle of secession, as minority ethnic groups seek their own sovereignty and independence.

The fires of conflict are often further stoked by the media, which lavishes glory and attention on independence movements. To fight for freedom is an honor. For every Palestinian who has killed an Israeli, there are hundreds of Kashmiris, Tamils, and Bosnians eager to shoot at their enemies. Newspapers, television and radio news broadcasts, and other media play a vital part in fomenting that sense of honor. They magnify each crisis, glorify rebellion, and help to feed the fire of conflict.

The third factor behind increasing conflict in the world is the social and geographic mobility that modern society enjoys. We can move anywhere we want and can aspire—or so we believe—to be anything we wish. Every day the television tantalizingly dangles the prizes that life can offer. We all want our share. But increased mobility and ambition also mean increased competition, which leads to antagonism. Antagonism often fastens itself to ethnic, racial, or religious differences. If you are an inner-city African American and your local grocer happens to be Korean American, you may see that individual as different from yourself—an intruder—rather than as a person, a neighbor, or a grocer. This same feeling of "us" versus "them" has been part of many an ethnic conflict around the world.

Many conflicts have been contained—even solved—by wise, responsible leadership. But unfortunately, many politicians use citizens' discontent for their own ends. They incite hatred, manipulate voters, and mobilize people against their neighbors. The worst things happen when neighbor turns against neighbor. In Bosnia, in Rwanda, in Lebanon, and in countless other places, people who had lived and worked together and had even intermarried went on a rampage, killing, raping, and robbing one another with gusto. If the appalling carnage teaches us anything, it is that we should stop seeing one another as hostile competitors and enemies and accept one another as people. Most importantly, we should learn to understand why conflicts happen and how they can be prevented. That is why *World in Conflict* is so important—the books in this series will help you understand the history and inner dynamics of some of the most persistent conflicts of modern times. And understanding is the first step to prevention. ⊕

INTRODUCTION

For several decades, Northern Ireland—a **province** within the United Kingdom—has been beset by what are sometimes called "the troubles." Troubles, an expression picked up by the media and widely used, describes mildly what in reality is a long, slow war between two populations that have long been divided by **ethnicity,** religion, and history. Almost the entire population of Northern Ireland belongs to either the Catholic or the Protestant faith. In stories covering the struggles of Northern Ireland, the media often choose the labels "Protestant" and "Catholic" as a shortcut to distinguish the conflict's participants.

After reading such reports, one might think that the problems in Northern Ireland result from two incompatible religions trying to exist within one society. Yet in other parts of the world, including the United States, Catholics and Protestants live together peacefully. A closer look at the issues reveals that the sources of the conflict are much more complicated.

POLITICAL GEOGRAPHY

The difficulties of Northern Ireland become more clear by looking at its geography. Northern Ireland takes up one-sixth of the Irish island. The Republic of Ireland (the Republic) occupies the remaining five-sixths and borders Northern Ireland on the south and on the northwest. The Irish island is one of the British Isles, a grouping that includes Great Britain. England, Scotland, and Wales, all on the island of Great Britain, make up the rest of the United Kingdom.

Northern Ireland sits west of England. Over many centuries, England ruled various parts of the Irish island. By settling on the island, particularly in what is present-day Northern Ireland, the English played a major role in creating the demographics (the makeup of the population) that shape the current conflict.

The six counties that make up Northern Ireland lie in the northeastern corner of the Irish island, which also includes the Republic of Ireland. Even the name of the province causes division. Protestants in Northern Ireland favor the historic term "Ulster," because it suggests an identity separate from the region's Irishness. Catholics prefer "the north" or "the six counties" to emphasize the connection between Northern Ireland and the rest of the island.

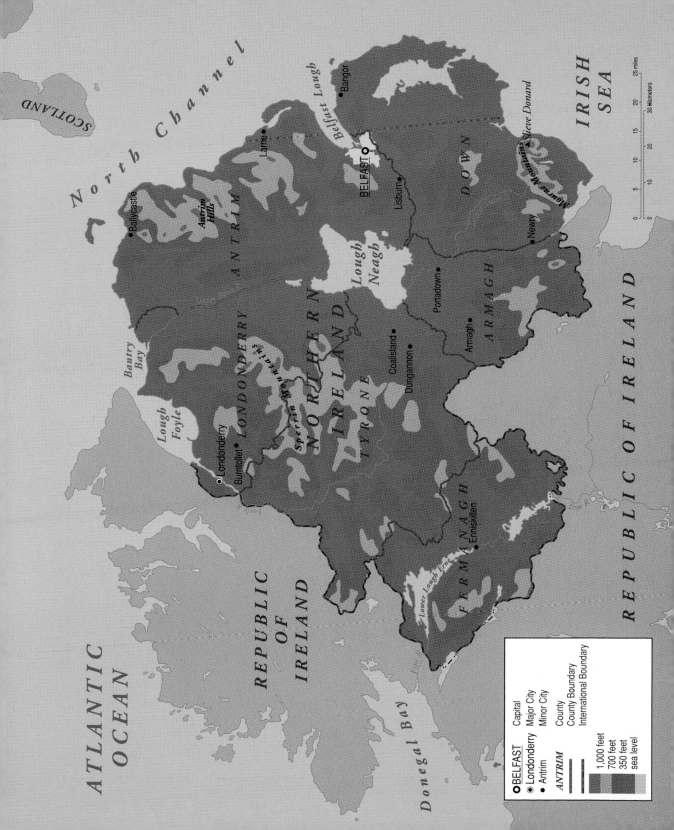

Sheep graze along the coast of County Antrim.

Geographic Facts about Northern Ireland

Northern Ireland comprises six counties: Antrim, Armagh, Londonderry, Down, Fermanagh, and Tyrone. Together they occupy 5,452 square miles, about the size of Connecticut. Coastline, which surrounds much of this small province, gave rise to Northern Ireland's shipbuilding and fishing industries. The rugged northern coast in County Antrim is particularly known for its beauty. Lough Neagh, the largest lake in the British Isles, occupies the center of the province. The Bann River flows through the lake, entering from the south as the Upper Bann and exiting at the northwest as the Lower Bann. Other major river systems are the Foyle and the Erne. Livestock and crop farming occupy the lowlands of Northern Ireland's central region. Relatively low mountains with rounded peaks, the Sperrin Mountains, rise in the northwestern counties of Tyrone and Londonderry. Northern Ireland's Mourne Mountains lie on the southeastern coast. This jagged range contains Slieve Donard, the highest peak in the province. (The Gaelic word for mountain is slieve.)

For centuries, the Irish island was one country, Ireland, even when it was ruled by outsiders. Northern Ireland was formerly part of a nine-county region known as Ulster. Only in the 1920s did Britain determine that six of the nine counties should have a separate status from the rest of the Irish island. The majority of the population living in these six counties was Protestant and chose to remain under British rule. When Britain carved away this portion of Ulster and joined it constitutionally with Great Britain, the official name became the United Kingdom of Great Britain and Northern Ireland. The population on the rest of the island, the modern Republic, was almost entirely Catholic and fought to become self-governing.

In the Republic's constitution, its government also claims ultimate **sovereignty** over the six northern counties. The constitution states that the "national territory" includes the entire island. The Republic of Ireland doesn't insist, however, that its constitution be applied to Northern Ireland, acknowledging that those six northeastern counties first must be "reintegrated."

THE MAJORITY'S WISHES

For years the British government has maintained that it would give up control of Northern Ireland if such a change was approved by a majority of the province's 1.6 million residents. The government of the Republic has expressed a willingness to amend its constitution, removing its claim on the six counties if such a change were part of an overall settlement of the Northern Ireland conflict.

Since the province's founding, the majority of Northern Ireland's people has always been Protestant. But the population's composition has changed over several decades. In 1920, when Northern Ireland was created, its population was about 67 percent Protestant. That figure has dropped to under 60 percent. The Catholic population has increased to 42 percent. Because Catholics tend to have larger families than Protestants, some experts estimate that in the first half of the twenty-first century, Catholics will outnumber Protes-

tants in the province. The shifting demographics have unnerved some Protestants. They fear that a Catholic majority in Northern Ireland will dissolve ties with the United Kingdom and will reunite with the Republic, which has an almost entirely Catholic population.

THE FUNDAMENTAL ISSUE

Protestants and Catholics both inhabit Northern Ireland, but they view themselves as quite separate culturally. If asked their **nationality,** most Catholics call themselves Irish, while the majority of Protestants call themselves British.

Corrugated walls and barbed wire separate Catholic and Protestant areas of Belfast, the capital of Northern Ireland.

Almost all Protestants wish to retain Northern Ireland's place in the United Kingdom. About one-quarter of the province's Catholics express a strong desire to see Northern Ireland united with the Republic. The divided vision over Northern Ireland's future is the fundamental issue that shapes politics in the province.

On one side are the Irish "nationalists," also sometimes called "republicans." Nationalist groups tend to be made up almost entirely of Catholics. Nationalists believe the six counties that were formerly a part of Ulster should be united with the Republic. Most nationalists want to bring about unification through political means. But within this Catholic population is a small group that believes so strongly in reunification it is willing to use force to make it happen. This element of the Catholic population has spawned several **paramilitary** organizations to advance its cause. Members of these groups have participated in assassinations and bombing missions on the Irish island and in Great Britain. Most well known among the nationalist paramilitaries is the Provisional Irish Republican Army (PIRA).

On the other side of the Northern Ireland conflict is a predominantly Protestant group whose members are usually called "loyalists" or "unionists" because they favor the continued union between Britain and Northern Ireland. Presbyterians of Scottish origin and Anglicans of English descent constitute most of Northern Ireland's Protestant population, and these groups immigrated to the island between three and five centuries ago. During that time, England intentionally created a loyalist, Protestant majority in Ulster. Never governed by a Catholic majority, most of the Protestants who live in Northern Ireland hope they never will be.

Similar to the extreme element of the Catholic population that uses force to try to reunite Ireland, the Protestant community also has a faction with organized paramilitary groups. These organizations are willing to use force to keep Northern Ireland part of the United Kingdom. The biggest of the Protestant paramilitary groups is the Ulster Defense Association (UDA).

SEGREGATION

During the centuries that the British and the Irish have shared the island, the level of tension between the two populations has fluctuated. The wave of violence that began in the late 1960s heightened people's awareness of their ethnicity. To most outsiders, British people and Irish people do not seem to come from such very distinct roots. Scientists say no real genetic difference exists. Members of the groups involved, however, believe they can generally tell

> *"In every way you were brought up to feel there were people called Catholics who you shouldn't have anything to do with. That wasn't difficult: you didn't know any and never met any. . . . No one ever told you what was so terrible about them."*

Paramilitary Organizations

The term "paramilitary" often refers to unofficial, underground groups that are organized like armies and that engage in unconventional methods of fighting. Illegal and violent groups have sprung up among both the extreme nationalists and the extreme loyalists in Northern Ireland.

On the nationalist side, the PIRA—committed to forcing the British out of the province—consists of about 400 active guerrilla fighters. A number of smaller nationalist paramilitary groups exist, including the Irish National Liberation Army (INLA), which is so militant that PIRA members call those involved with INLA "wildmen."

Loyalists formed the UDA in the early 1970s. UDA defenders claimed that violence was not the fundamental purpose of the group. In 1992 the government declared that the UDA was "actively and primarily" engaged in terrorism and outlawed the group. While it was legal, the UDA had a huge membership—perhaps 40,000 at its peak in the early 1970s—among working-class Protestants. Only a small portion of its members was involved in paramilitary activities. The Ulster Volunteer Force (UVF) and other smaller loyalist paramilitary organizations are also on the list of banned organizations.

A member of a paramilitary group

one another apart using clues, such as family name, accent, or subtle differences of appearance, dress, and style. Although none of these methods is totally reliable, they point to each group's need to see itself as distinct from the other.

Over recent decades, the split in cultural loyalty between the two communities has been accompanied by an increasing physical separation in housing, education, and other areas of life. Fear of attack by paramilitary forces of the other group—or fear of retaliation by extreme members of one's own side for intermixing—forced people to distinguish themselves according to religion and ethnicity.

During the early years of violence, people moved to neighborhoods where they felt safer, so neighborhoods in which both Catholics and Protestants lived became rare. In fact, in some cities, the government constructed peace lines—walls that physically separate Catholic neighborhoods from adjoining Protestant neighborhoods. Almost all neighborhoods in present-day Northern Ireland are segregated by ethnicity—most neighborhoods are more than 90 percent Catholic or Protestant. Only 2 percent of grammar school students attend schools that could be called integrated.

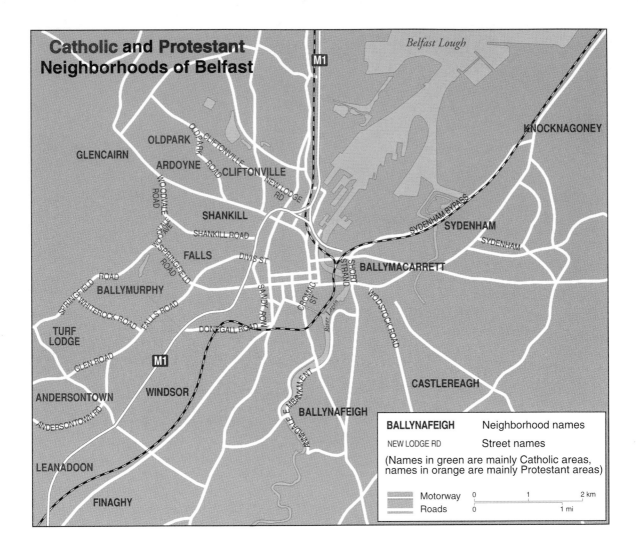

Catholic and Protestant Neighborhoods of Belfast

Major social institutions, such as civic clubs and sports teams, have either Catholic or Protestant membership and are seldom open to mixed membership. Many Protestants and Catholics grow up in Northern Ireland without meeting people of the other faith as neighbors, classmates, social acquaintances, or business associates.

Although tensions between those who consider themselves Irish and those who consider themselves British exist throughout Northern Ireland, much of the violence has occurred in urban areas, where two-thirds of the province's population resides. Major episodes of the conflict have occurred in Belfast and Londonderry, the two largest cities. Belfast (population about 284,000) is the capital and largest city in Northern Ireland, home to about one-fifth of the province's population. With about two-thirds of Belfast's population belonging to the Protestant community, the city remains a long-time loyalist stronghold. But in a few neighborhoods, particularly in west Belfast, almost all residents are Catholic.

The composition of Londonderry's population (about 63,000) is just the opposite of Belfast's. Catholics outnumber Protestants in Londonderry by two to one. Protestants who do live in Londonderry reside in the few neighborhoods where Catholic citizens are scarce.

NORTHERN IRELAND'S ECONOMY

Until the industrial revolution in the middle of the eighteenth century, most people in what is modern Northern Ireland depended on agriculture for their livelihood. With the introduction of new technology, shipbuilding and linen manufacturing thrived and drew many rural people to the cities, especially to the port cities of Belfast and Londonderry, in search of work.

Agriculture, linen manufacturing, and shipbuilding formed the basis of the economy for many decades. Agriculture has since decreased and accounts for less than 10 percent of jobs in the workforce. Potatoes and barley are the biggest crops. Farmers also raise cattle, sheep, hogs, and especially poultry. Linen manufacturing, which uses flax grown on the island, has also declined. Much of the textile industry produces fabrics from synthetic materials. About 20 percent of the jobs in Northern Ireland are in manufacturing.

Private service industries employ growing numbers of people. A small but increasing portion of the population works in tourism, an industry that has been hampered by civil unrest. The government is the biggest sector of the economy, employing hundreds of thousands and providing benefits to almost everyone. Government expenditures account for more than 50 percent of Northern Ireland's economy.

Because of social programs funded by the British government, the average citizen of Northern Ireland is more prosperous than the average person in the Republic is. Yet the average citizen of England, Scotland, or Wales—the other parts of the United Kingdom—has a higher standard of living than does the average person in Northern Ireland.

ECONOMIC DISCRIMINATION

Analyzing the prosperity of Northern Ireland's population by ethnic or religious group uncovers another source of grudges. In fact, some observers of the conflict believe that economic

> "People sometimes think it's a Catholic-Protestant thing, a religious problem. But that's simplistic. Other people would like to think that it's a colonial, imperial problem, that if you get the British out of Northern Ireland, all will be well. That's a myth."
> Mairead Corrigan Maguire,
> Co-founder, Community of the Peace People

factors, more than religious or ethnic differences, perpetuate the problems in Northern Ireland.

Protestants enjoy a disproportionate share of the province's wealth. In the past, blatant legal **discrimination** maintained these inequalities. Beginning in the sixteenth century, the British government took land from Irish Catholics and gave it to Protestants lured from England and Scotland by the opportunity to be landlords. (Although some immigrants became wealthy landowners, many immigrants arrived on the Irish island as bonded servants and tenant farmers.) The penal laws of the eighteenth century banned Catholics from buying land, from entering professions, from receiving a formal education, from serving in government, or from voting in parliamentary elections.

Laws have since banned discrimination against Catholics, and the economic gap between Protestants and Catholics has closed to some extent. To address unfair hiring practices, the British government instituted a policy requiring employers in larger businesses to hire Catholics and Protestants in the proportions reflected in the local population. This policy caused resentment among unemployed and underemployed Protestants, who felt they lost jobs for which they traditionally would have been hired.

Hostility between the groups endures, causing Catholics to feel frozen out

High unemployment, especially among young Catholic men, is one of Northern Ireland's biggest problems. One father complains, "You take my Brendan now, 24 years of age and's never had a day's work in his life. . . . What sort of a life's that for a young man?"

© Bruce Haley

Some members of paramilitary groups, including the illegal Provisional Irish Republican Army (PIRA), beat up those who socialize with people of the other religion.

© Belfast Telegraph Newspapers Ltd.

of many areas of economic opportunity in ways that are more subtle than in the past. According to Catholics, discrimination still results in higher unemployment rates and lower incomes for Catholic citizens. The unemployment rate among Catholic men and women is more than double the rate among Protestant men and women.

ONGOING CONFLICT

Ethnic conflict takes different shapes around the world. Race, religion, ethnic background, language, or other cultural differences often separate the groups in conflict. Many times, the conflict erupts in reaction to a history of discrimination. All of these factors enter into the troubles in Northern Ireland, mixed in a way that gives the conflict its distinct character.

Although religion is the shortcut many observers use to describe the source of conflict in Northern Ireland, history reveals that religion was not always a factor. The conflict on the Irish island existed even when England and Ireland were both Catholic countries. And in the early stages of the struggle for Irish independence and equality, the leaders of the Irish nationalist cause were more often Protestants than Catholics. Bear in mind, too, that in modern times freedom of religion is guaranteed for both groups.

Yet most of those who call themselves unionists and British are Protestants and have been raised with the belief that they are superior to Catholics. Most of those who call themselves nationalists and Irish are Catholics and feel an urge to avenge grudges both ancient and recent. The most extreme elements in both groups find these differences worth fighting about.

MAJOR PLAYERS IN THE CONFLICT

British Army

DUP Emblem

The Republic

Adams, Gerry   Leader of Sinn Féin since 1983 and spokesperson for the illegal Provisional Irish Republican Army.

British Army   Troops have patrolled Northern Ireland since 1969, when Britain took charge of security after the province's Protestant-dominated forces proved they couldn't provide unbiased protection.

Democratic Unionist Party (DUP)   Founded by Ian Paisley in 1971. The DUP believes Protestants have the democratic right to run the province. The party wants to maintain strong ties with Britain and opposes power-sharing with the Republic of Ireland.

Hume, John   A founder of the Social Democratic and Labour Party and party leader since 1979.

Irish Republican Army (IRA)   See PIRA.

Molyneaux, James   Leader of the Ulster Unionist Party from 1979 until his resignation in 1995.

Northern Ireland Civil Rights Association (NICRA)   Founded in 1967 to obtain equality for Catholics through nonviolent protest.

Paisley, Ian   Leader of the Democratic Unionist Party since 1971.

Provisional Irish Republican Army (PIRA)   Sinn Féin's military arm, the PIRA is Northern Ireland's largest nationalist paramilitary group. Oftentimes the PIRA is called the IRA. The IRA splintered in 1969 into the PIRA and the Official IRA.

Republic of Ireland (the Republic) Proclaims ultimate sovereignty over Northern Ireland but will relinquish the claim as part of an overall settlement. The Anglo-Irish Agreement gave the Republic a power-sharing role in the province.

Royal Ulster Constabulary (RUC) Northern Ireland's provincewide police force. The RUC hires mostly Protestants. During the late 1960s, the RUC showed favoritism toward Protestants, so Britain sent troops to protect Catholic citizens.

Sinn Féin Emblem

Sinn Féin Pronounced "shin fayn" and formed in 1905. The political wing of the PIRA, Sinn Féin attracts Catholic voters who believe so strongly in a united Ireland that they justify the use of terrorism.

Social Democratic and Labour Party (SDLP) Established in 1970. Calling itself the reconciliation party, the SDLP encourages membership from both religious groups. However, the goal of uniting Ireland with the majority's consent steers away many Protestants.

SDLP Emblem

Ulster Defense Association (UDA) Formed in the 1970s to protect Protestants from nationalist terrorists. Northern Ireland's largest loyalist paramilitary group, the UDA was legal until 1992.

Ulster Defense Regiment (UDR) Established in 1970. This British army regiment recruits members, most of whom are Protestant, from Northern Ireland.

UUP Emblem

Ulster Unionist Party (UUP) Founded in 1898, the root for several parties formed in the 1960s and 1970s. The UUP still attracts many Protestants who want to keep ties to Britain using nonviolent means.

 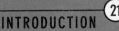

CHAPTER

1

THE RECENT CONFLICT AND ITS EFFECTS

For many years, practically every international news story about Northern Ireland has been about the fighting or about efforts to end the fighting in this corner of the Irish island. Quite understandably, the outside world thinks of Northern Ireland as a war zone. Once in a while, a reporter points out that traffic accidents cause more deaths in Northern Ireland than violence does. And a single incident in other long-standing conflicts, such as those in Rwanda, Bosnia, Sudan, and East Timor, has sometimes resulted in more deaths than the Irish conflict has caused in decades.

In recent years, the media have also created the false impression that most ordinary citizens back the violent activities of Northern Ireland's paramilitary groups. Polls have shown that a huge majority of Protestants favors continuing Northern Ireland's connection with Britain and that a solid portion of Catholics supports the goal of uniting Ireland. (Although a substantial number of Catholics wish to remain part of the United Kingdom for economic reasons, many of these belong to nationalist political parties because of the parties' stances on other issues.) The future constitutional status that the political parties want—backed by each reli-

In July 1996, rioters set fire to vehicles along Sandy Row, a mainly Protestant area of Belfast. Violence erupted when demonstrators supporting a Protestant parade clashed with members of the Royal Ulster Constabulary (RUC), who were trying to stop the march from going through a Catholic area.

© Alan Lewis/Sygma

gious population's majority—corresponds with the status the paramilitary groups of each ethnic-religious community want. Neither the Catholic nor the Protestant majority, however, supports paramilitary violence to achieve the differing goals for Northern Ireland's future.

VOTERS REJECT VIOLENCE

A breakdown of voting patterns reflects the population's opposition to violence. The two biggest Catholic parties are Sinn Féin, known as "the political wing of the Provisional IRA," and the Social Democratic and Labour Party (SDLP). The SDLP, which repudiates the PIRA and the use of force, has pledged to work for unification by peaceful means. So in choosing between the two main nationalist parties, Catholic voters have a clear means of indicating whether they approve of the PIRA's campaign of violence. The SDLP always outpolls Sinn Féin, usually by a margin of about two to one.

Although Sinn Féin draws less support from Northern Ireland's Catholic voters than the SDLP, the party receives more attention in

Gerry Adams

Sinn Féin leader since 1983, Gerry Adams is the most visible face of Irish nationalism. Adams comes from a long line of Republicans. His mother grew up in a legendary Republican family, and his father was shot and imprisoned in the cause. While still in his teens, Adams joined Sinn Féin, which was then an illegal political party. Since legalized, Sinn Féin is often described as the political arm of the PIRA.

The PIRA is an illegal organization and membership is a crime. Adams has never admitted to belonging to the PIRA. British Intelligence authorities, however, believe he was a high-ranking PIRA leader in the 1970s, and under an antiterrorist policy, the government imprisoned him without charges several times throughout the decade. The government didn't find enough evidence to charge Adams with PIRA-related crimes and eventually released him.

In his role of Sinn Féin leader, Adams maintains a slight distance from the PIRA. For example, he sometimes criticizes those PIRA actions that result in the death of innocent civilians. But when British troops are targeted, Adams describes PIRA members as "freedom fighters" who have a right to "engage in resistance." When other political parties focus on PIRA violence as the root of Northern Ireland's problems, Adams always reframes the issue and declares that the causes are the British presence and the unjust division of the Irish island.

To his foes Adams is the symbol of terrorism, but he has become indispensable to the peace process. Some believe that the historic breakthroughs toward peace in the mid-1990s began in April 1993 with Adams's secret talks with the SDLP. Although his apparent willingness to participate in all-party talks is hopeful, no one knows to what degree Adams controls the actions of the PIRA.

> *"An article recently in the [London] Daily Mirror listed the names of the 2,750 people killed [to date] in the Troubles. I must know 20 or 30 of them. The list was in the shape of a cross. The first name I came to that I knew was A. J. Hannigan, my grandmother."*

the international news because of its connection with the PIRA. Sinn Féin leader Gerry Adams is the public face of the PIRA, although it is not clear whether Adams actually has any authority over the PIRA's fighters. Membership in the PIRA is illegal, and those who join are considered wanted criminals by the British authorities. Sinn Féin is a legal political party whose top officials, to stay out of prison themselves, must not acknowledge too close a connection to the PIRA.

Protestants' voting patterns also reflect an objection to violence. The moderate Ulster Unionist Party (UUP), which disapproves of violence, always outpolls the militant Democratic Unionist Party (DUP). Although the majority of Northern Ireland's citizens vote for parties that support settling differences through peaceful, democratic means, a minority of those within each ethnic-religious community can keep the war going.

WHO ARE THE VICTIMS?

In the first years after 1969, the year most observers consider the start of the recent conflict in Northern Ireland, much of the violence occurred during riots. The nationalists or the loyalists organized public demonstrations. Elements of the other community would try to disrupt the event or would organize a counterdemonstration. The two mobs would come into contact, and violence would flare. Sometimes the riots pitted the police against Catholic demonstrators. British army troops arrived in 1969 to keep the peace, but the violence continued and soon in-

volved the troops as well. Some citizens who simply turned out for rallies, and even some who withdrew to their homes to avoid danger, fell victim to random violence in those years.

In more recent years, this pattern of mass rioting has decreased, and aggression by paramilitary groups has become more focused. The PIRA has attacked the Royal Ulster Constabulary (RUC, Northern Ireland's police), the Ulster Defense Regiment (UDR, a locally recruited regiment of the British army), or British troops. Protestant paramilitaries have gone after suspected key members (either paramilitary or political) of the nationalist movement. Both Catholic and Protestant paramilitary groups have attacked members of their own ethnic-religious communities whom the militant groups perceive as having betrayed them. The PIRA also attempts to police Catholic neighborhoods by administering warnings, beatings, and even "kneecappings" (breaking or maiming a person's knees by gunshot or with sticks or bricks) to punish suspected petty crimi-

In November 1987, a hearse carrying the body of Marie Wilson passed in front of the bombed remains of Enniskillen's community center. While watching a parade honoring soldiers who had died in World War I, Wilson and 10 others were killed when a PIRA bomb exploded.

nals. This is consistent with the PIRA's refusal to view Northern Ireland as a Protestant-run province of the United Kingdom. The PIRA sees itself, therefore, as the only legitimate law enforcement authority.

Although in general the paramilitaries have narrowed the focus of their attacks since the early 1970s, sometimes paramilitary groups kill civilians at random. Catholics in nationalist neighborhoods or Protestants in loyalist neighborhoods can become

targets of paramilitary attacks carried out in retaliation for previous violence by the other community's paramilitary groups. In addition,

paramilitary groups sometimes make mistakes and kill the wrong people. In the late 1980s, the PIRA conducted a number of bombings that

Between 1969 and the early 1990s, 3,000 people died and more than 35,000 others were wounded in Northern Ireland's conflict. While the actual numbers may seem relatively small, the impact the violence has had on Northern Ireland's population is large. In the province of 1.6 million people, one in six households has had a member injured or killed. As a comparison, if a conflict were happening on the same scale in the United States, where the population is much greater, the number killed would be 400,000 and the number injured would be 3 million.

they admitted did not go as planned. Bombs went off early or in the wrong direction, and innocent victims were killed. For instance, a PIRA bomb planted on a school bus was intended to kill the driver, who was a member of the UDA. But the bomb exploded early, injuring many of the schoolchildren.

During much of the conflict, the government attributed most killings to the PIRA or to smaller nationalist paramilitaries, such as the Irish National Liberation Army. But the loyalist side also wages its own campaign of terror. The two biggest loyalist paramilitaries, the UDA and the Ulster Volunteer Force (UVF), conduct violent missions to maintain Northern Ireland's status as part of the United Kingdom. And in the early 1990s, the RUC attributed more deaths to the loyalists than to the nationalists.

THE CONFLICT'S LARGE SHADOW

Although the odds that an ordinary person in Northern Ireland will die as a direct result of the violence are relatively low, the conflict nonetheless has cast a large shadow over daily life. Everyone lives with the constant presence of army troops, whose officially stated purpose is to keep order and to protect all Northern Ireland citizens. Soldiers carry rifles while they patrol the streets. In some areas, especially in Belfast and Londonderry, troops routinely dress for battle, wearing metal helmets and bulletproof jackets.

Moreover, many basic rights have been curtailed.

In Londonderry members of the Ulster Defense Association (UDA), an illegal Protestant paramilitary group, stand guard over a British flag.

© Ed Kashi

An ordinary resident of Northern Ireland—Protestant or Catholic—can be stopped and searched if soldiers think there's a chance the person is hiding a weapon or bomb. Roadblocks, set up to intercept vehicles transporting paramilitary weapons and ammunition, sometimes delay traffic for hours. Early in 1972, the British government disbanded Northern Ireland's Parliament and instituted direct rule. Ever since, a member of the British cabinet has governed the province from London, England, the British capital. Citizens of Northern Ireland do vote in nationwide parliamentary elections and send representatives to the House of Commons (Britain's Parliament).

In 1971, as part of its campaign to resolve Northern Ireland's problems, the British government suspended civil rights. Under the special rules of "internment," for example, a person in Northern Ireland suspected of terrorist activity could be held a long time without being formally charged with a crime. The suspect could be deprived of the right to consult a lawyer before being questioned and could be aggressively interrogated. (The British have often been accused of torturing suspects.) Such special powers have been invoked far more often against Catholics than they have against Protestants. The policy of

Imitating the world around them, boys in Belfast in the 1970s pretended to stop and search a passerby. The graffiti above the boys' heads calls for an end to Britain's internment policy.

internment caused fury among Northern Ireland's Catholics and condemnation among international civil rights groups. The British eventually discontinued it.

DEADLOCK

To the PIRA and other committed Irish nationalists, the presence of British troops, the implementation of direct rule, and the intermittent suspension of civil liberties all cast Britain as an unwanted foreign government occupying a portion of the Irish island. The PIRA has long maintained that the solution to Northern Ireland's problems would be the withdrawal of British troops and every other vestige of British control.

British leaders say they would like to reestablish self-rule in Northern Ireland, to reinstate normal citizens' rights, and to bring home British troops. These politicians have expressed interest in finding a way to permit the Republic to have some role in Northern Ireland. But partly because of threats made by Northern Ireland's

militant Protestants, who state they will carry out a civil war against Catholics if the British pull out, Great Britain remains in charge of the province.

As recently as 1992, attempts to end the fighting met with little success. Political breakthroughs led to a truce among all Northern Ireland paramilitary groups, beginning in the fall of 1994, that halted the fighting for 17 months. In February of 1996, however, the PIRA set off several bombs and interrupted the truce. More bombs and deaths have followed. The search for a long-term solution to the conflict continues. ⊕

After activities by the PIRA canceled the 17-month cease-fire in 1996, citizens of Northern Ireland gathered at a rally in Belfast. Holding white paper doves, the crowd voiced its desire for a return to peace.

© Paul Faith/Pacemaker Press International Ltd.

CHAPTER 1 *The Recent Conflict and Its Effects*

CHAPTER 2

THE CONFLICT'S ROOTS

The people whom the world thinks of as "Irish" have an age-old history. They descend from an ancient people known as the Celts. The Celts, who spread out from the area that is present-day Switzerland and southwestern Germany around 1000 B.C., populated many areas of Europe, including the British Isles. By 250 B.C., the Gaels, a subgroup of the Celts, landed in Ireland and settled there. The people of Ireland used the Gaelic language well into the nineteenth century.

Gaelic culture developed apart from the European mainstream because neither the Romans, who dominated western Europe in the early centuries A.D., nor Germanic tribes, who controlled the continent from the late fifth to the tenth centuries, came to Ireland. Gaelic Ireland was divided into five king-

Saint Patrick brought Christianity to Ireland in the fifth century.

Archive Photos

doms and hundreds of smaller political units called *tuatha*. The kingdom of Ulaid, which later came to be called Ulster, occupied most of the northern part of the island. The kingdoms and the tuatha frequently fought one another.

CHRISTIANS AND VIKINGS

For centuries Gaelic culture flourished under priestlike leaders called Druids. In A.D. 432 Patrick, a Christian missionary from Great Britain, arrived in Ireland. He converted many of the Irish to Catholicism, uprooting the ancient Druidic religion. Patrick, who eventually became bishop of Ireland, emphasized the importance of education and built the Cathedral Church in Armagh as an institution for Christian teaching.

Starting in the late 700s and continuing for the next

ence of the Vikings. The Gaelic name for the island, Éire, is combined with "land," a Viking term.

Eventually, the tuatha began banding together to fight the invaders. By 1014 the Irish had defeated the Vikings in the Battle of Clontarf, losing their leader, Brian Boru, in the fighting. The Viking invasions ended, but

two centuries, Viking invaders from Norway sailed to Ireland. They killed farmers, stole valuable religious objects, and destroyed religious buildings. But some of the invaders stayed on and established Ireland's first permanent towns. For example, the Vikings founded Dublin, the capital of the present-day Republic, in 841. The newcomers also established Limerick, Cork, and Waterford. In fact, the name *Ireland* reflects the influ-

Left: *Among the first groups to invade the Irish island were Viking sailors from Norway. Beginning in the late eighth century, they sailed from their homes in northern Europe to loot Christian churches and monasteries. Irish efforts to repel the attacks finally succeeded in the Battle of Clontarf in 1014. During the fight (above), a Viking killed Brian Boru, the Irish king.*

Irish monks created ornate copies of the Christian Gospels, such as the Book of Kells (left), that have distinctly Irish decorations.

of modern Italy, France, and Germany. Because of Ireland's isolation from mainland Europe, however, Irish Christianity had developed its own practices. These differed in several respects from the rules followed in Rome, the center of the Roman Catholic Church. For example, priests in Ireland could be married, and laymen could serve as abbots (heads of monasteries). These differences bothered the pope, the Church's leader.

In 1155, to bring Ireland into line with Catholic norms, Pope Adrian IV issued a decree. It granted King Henry II of England lordship over Ireland, providing that he used his authority "to reveal the truth of the Christian faith to the peoples still untaught and barbarous." Despite the decree, Henry didn't immediately take up the pope's offer.

those who had already settled in Ireland stayed, becoming part of the culture.

Although the Vikings had attacked monasteries and other religious sites, Ireland remained a stronghold of Christianity. Many Christian scholars from Europe took refuge on the island to avoid persecution by the Germanic tribes who had overrun parts

NORMANS FROM ENGLAND

Although the pope had granted Henry II the power to rule Ireland, the Irish kingdoms still existed and still fought one another. In the 1160s, a small kingdom in southeastern Ireland ruled by Dermot MacMurrough was taken over by another Irish kingdom. MacMurrough sought King Henry's help.

Henry, along with the rest of the English ruling class, descended from the Normans, who had conquered England in the eleventh century. MacMurrough encouraged King Henry to allow Norman nobles to aid him in his effort to regain the lost territory. Henry agreed. He reasoned that a Norman army could help colonize the island, making it more English and more Roman Catholic.

In return for their military services, the Normans would receive from MacMurrough some of the land they recovered. Within a few years, several Norman nobles had established themselves as owners of estates in Ireland. Henry II grew concerned that these nobles, who were supposed to be loyal to him, were setting up an independent power base.

In 1171 King Henry chose to remind the Irish, as well as the Normans, that he was the lord of Ireland. Henry dusted off the papal decree and invaded Ireland, the first clash in the long struggle between England and Ireland. Officially, the English conquest succeeded. But the English found they couldn't control much of Ireland outside of Dublin and the surrounding area. Fighting continued throughout the island. Furthermore, many of the Normans previously sent to colonize Ireland had adopted the native Gaelic language and customs rather than establishing English culture. Some took the Irish side and fought against England.

In response, the English established various laws and policies to widen and strengthen their authority. The Statutes of Kilkenny, for example, outlawed intermarriage between the Irish and the English and banned the use of the Gaelic language. The Irish interpreted the statutes, which existed from 1366 to 1613, as demeaning to their culture. And the English kings still found that the outlook of whomever they sent to run Ireland seemed to become more Irish than English. Henry VII tried to enforce loyalty from the English rulers of Ireland when in 1495 he imposed Poynings' Law, under which the Irish Parliament could meet only with the advance approval of the king and any laws had to be approved by the king and his councillors.

THE PROTESTANT CHURCH

Religion became an aspect of the Anglo-Irish dispute in

In 1155, to bring Ireland into line with Catholic norms, Pope Adrian IV issued a decree. It granted King Henry II of England lordship over Ireland, providing that he used his authority "to reveal the truth of the Christian faith to the peoples still untaught and barbarous."

1533. At that time, King Henry VIII rebelled against Roman Catholicism for political reasons. He established the Anglican Church as the official religion of England and tried to set up a similar institution in Ireland, too. In the new church, whose followers were called Protestants, the king of England replaced the pope as the ultimate authority. Most Irish remained loyal to the Roman Catholic Church.

In another aggressive move, Henry VIII put in place a policy known as the surrender and regrant laws, which were intended to establish a more loyal relationship with Ireland. Surrender and regrant required landowners to surrender all land titles to the king. If the landowners then took an oath of loyalty to him, the king might—but wasn't obliged to—regrant the titles. This approach didn't earn the king much real loyalty, and the Irish outside of the Dublin region widely resisted the policy.

Henry's son, King Edward VI, launched military campaigns from Dublin to drive off their land those who had resisted surrender and regrant. He installed English and Scottish immigrants who were already loyal. These new settlers leased the land from the king at favorable rents. Under "plantation," as this practice was known, the king "planted" his imported loyalists on large farms. During his reign, Edward declared that Protestantism was the official religion of Ireland.

In the decades that followed, the English continued to forcefully control

Mansell Collection/Time, Inc.

An illustration showing England's Henry VIII crushing Pope Clement is intended to symbolize the king's rejection of Roman Catholicism and the formation of the new Anglican Church.

Family Ties

The kingdoms of Europe had long held to the custom of preferring that male family members inherit the royal throne. Women, it was thought, didn't have the strength or wisdom to govern. As a result, producing male descendants was of huge importance. In the case of the Tudor family, which ruled England and Ireland from the late 1400s to the early 1600s, efforts to ensure male successors had a lasting effect on both countries.

Henry VIII felt his dynasty was at risk because his only surviving legitimate child was his daughter Mary. He tried to get permission from the Catholic Church to divorce his wife, but the Church refused. Henry's response was to break with the Church, to declare himself head of a new Protestant church, and to grant himself a divorce. With wife number two Henry had another daughter, Elizabeth, and with wife number three a long-awaited son, Edward. (No children resulted from his last three marriages.)

Henry's efforts to ensure the succession and to keep England Protestant spawned more than he could ever have predicted. Edward VI, author of the plantation system, sent thousands of Protestants to Ireland to dilute the island's Catholic culture. Edward

National Portrait Gallery, London

Queen Elizabeth I

died young and had no children. Although a Catholic, Edward's sister Mary inherited and launched England into a period of anti-Protestant unrest. At Mary's death in 1558, Elizabeth took over, ruling England and Ireland as a Protestant queen for 45 years. She continued Edward's plantation policy and enacted several anti-Catholic measures.

landownership through the plantation policy. Queen Elizabeth I, Edward's sister, carried on the policy when she inherited the throne in 1558. She also outlawed Catholic religious services. Under her rule, some Roman Catholic priests and bishops were executed. Catholics continued to worship but had to do so in secret.

CATHOLIC UPRISINGS

Ulster, the biggest and most successful of all the regions that had managed to resist English influence, became the heart of Gaelic civilization. With the exception of the coastal counties of Antrim and Down, where plantation Scots had established farms, Ulster remained almost untouched by English influence in the 1500s.

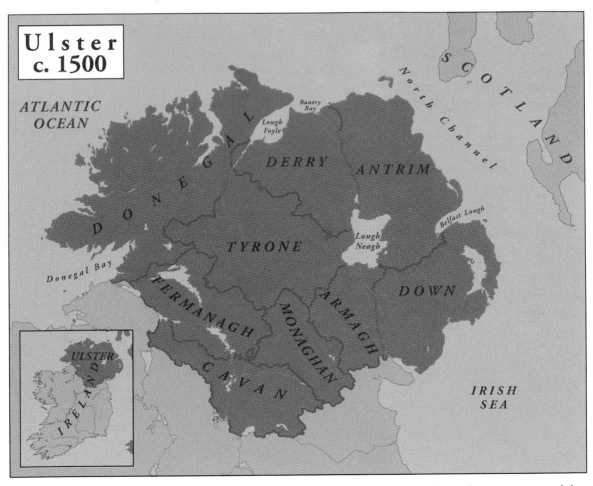

**Ulster
c. 1500**

ATLANTIC
OCEAN

*Lough
Foyle*

*Bantry
Bay*

DERRY

ANTRIM

S C O T L A N D

North Channel

D O N E G A L

TYRONE

*Lough
Neagh*

Belfast Lough

DOWN

Donegal Bay

FERMANAGH

MONAGHAN

ARMAGH

ULSTER

IRELAND

C A V A N

IRISH
SEA

The historic region of Ulster, an early Irish kingdom, consisted of nine counties in the northeastern portion of the Irish island. The nine-county area, which had long resisted English influence, became the focus of England's "plantation" policy in the early 1600s.

In the late sixteenth century, two powerful Ulster landowners, Hugh O'Neill and Rory O'Donnell, led a major rebellion against English rule that lasted into the seventeenth century. The rebellion started in Ulster but quickly spread throughout Ireland. For a while, the rebel forces thrived. When Queen Elizabeth sent additional forces, Spain—England's enemy—agreed to help the Irish cause. The English troops defeated the Irish and Spanish troops in 1601.

Queen Elizabeth offered O'Neill and O'Donnell a chance to keep most of their lands if they submitted to English rule. They accepted in 1603, and the queen re-granted the land and gave them both the title of earl. By 1607 O'Neill, O'Donnell, and about a hundred other landowners who had made similar commitments with the English had found they couldn't keep the agreement and fled to France. This famous event, called the "flight of the earls," was crucial to the future development of Northern Ireland. By giving up their claim to a great deal of land, the earls enabled England to begin its biggest and most thorough experiment in plantation—the Ulster Plantation.

The London officials who planned the Ulster Plantation believed their idea wouldn't work if the new English landlords had to rely on Irish farmworkers. Instead, the officials wanted to bring in enough Protestant farmworkers from England and Scotland to outnumber the Irish. The plan would permit the Irish Catholics of Ulster to live only in specified areas, away from the best land. The new settlers would reside in English-speaking, Protestant-practicing communities that were loyal to England. The officials believed the settlers—

who came to be called Anglo-Scottish—would not absorb Irish culture because they wouldn't live among the Irish.

Although by 1620 the number of Anglo-Scottish in the region had soared to more than 20,000, the organizers found that the Ulster

lowing summer, the rebels were in control of most of Ireland outside of Dublin. In parts of Ulster, the rebels had massacred many thousands of Scottish and English planters.

The uprising of the 1640s occurred while England was engulfed in its own internal

English laws set up an "us-and-them" relationship between Anglo-Scottish Protestants and Irish Catholics.

Plantation needed still more workers. Displaced Irish farmers proved to be an easily acquired supply of labor. This solution to the labor shortage resulted in many Irish families renting or working as farmhands the land they had owned a few years earlier. Morever, English laws set up an "us-and-them" relationship between Anglo-Scottish Protestants and Irish Catholics. To the Irish, such policies reflected the English attitude that the Irish were subhuman.

Resentments boiled over and resulted in another major uprising that began in Ulster in 1641. By the fol-

struggle between supporters of the king and supporters of a radical Parliament headed by Oliver Cromwell. After gaining control of England, Cromwell led a large army into Ireland in 1649. By 1650 Cromwell had regained most of the island except Connaught—a province in the west—and the surrounding area.

Cromwell imposed a harsh peace, slaughtering many of those he had captured and exiling others to a slavelike existence in English colonies abroad. He abolished the Irish Parliament and forcibly took more than 11 million acres of land. Cromwell awarded estates and farms to soldiers and investors who had backed him in the war against the Irish. He banned the Irish from owning land in eastern Ireland. More than

After deposing Charles I, the king of England, Scotland, and Ireland, Oliver Cromwell (wearing blue sash) crushed an uprising in Ireland. Not long after Cromwell's death, Charles's Protestant son took back the kingdom, becoming Charles II.

40,000 Irish who'd been driven from this region fled to Connaught.

THE BATTLE OF THE BOYNE

By 1685 Catholics possessed only 22 percent of Ireland, although they still made up the vast majority of the population. In that year, however, England had run out of legitimate Protestant heirs for the throne. The country was forced to turn to the Catholic James Stuart, who became King James II. If James's reign had lasted, he might have restored some of the land and power to the dispossessed Catholics of Ireland. Instead, nervous Protestant nobles invited a Dutch Protestant prince, William of Orange, who had a more distant—but legal—claim, to take over the English throne. William forced James to flee to France in 1688—an event known in English history as the Glorious Revolution.

Seeking to regain his crown by controlling Ireland first, James landed in Ireland with a small French army in 1689. Most Irish Catholics backed James and were prepared to help him carry his campaign to England. They

fought not so much for an independent Ireland but for putting England and Ireland once again under a Catholic king.

To prevent his overthrow, William invaded Ireland—where all the action seemed to be taking place. The forces, drawn on religious lines, met north of Dublin at the Boyne River on July 1, 1690. William's army won. James fled to France and never set foot in England or Ireland again. In honor of William of Orange, the Protestants of Northern Ireland adopted orange as their symbolic color. (Even in modern times, some of Northern Ireland's Protestants belong to the Orange Order, whose members are known as Orangemen.)

PROTESTANT ASCENDANCY

After the Battle of the Boyne, the Protestant Ascendancy—as the ruling class in Ireland came to be called—controlled the re-established Irish Parliament and the Irish economy. William transferred even more land from Catholic to Protestant ownership. By the end of the 1600s, Catholics

In the late 1600s, Ireland became the setting for the Protestant-Catholic fight over the crown. Charles II had had no legitimate children, so his Catholic brother James (in front) *succeeded him. But Protestant nobles trusted neither James II nor his sympathy with the Catholics of Ireland. They asked William of Orange, a Protestant prince, to invade and force James from power. James tried to regain his crown on Irish soil, with support from the island's Catholic population. William won the Battle of the Boyne on July 1, 1690.*

Mansell Collection/Time, Inc.

books, and many remained in effect for the rest of the century. The laws banished Catholic bishops. No Catholic could possess any kind of weapon. A Catholic couldn't inherit land from a Protestant, couldn't buy land, and couldn't lease it for longer than 31 years. A Catholic couldn't enter a profession. They were banned from formal higher education, from the Irish and British Parliaments, from voting, and from teaching. Under these laws, landownership by Catholics dropped to 5 percent of the island.

Meanwhile, England had experienced its own changes. It ceased to be just England and became part of the political unit called Great Britain with the union of England and Scotland. In addition, by the mid-1700s, Great Britain was experiencing major advances in technology that allowed its industries to expand and become more efficient.

The industrial changes in Great Britain made their way to Ulster, especially to Belfast and Londonderry, where Protestants owned factories or managed them for British investors. Textile

held just 14 percent of the land. In 1695 the Protestant Ascendancy began enacting a series of anti-Catholic laws, known as penal laws, that assigned second-class status to Irish culture, language, and religion.

By 1728 all of the penal laws had been put on the

Born in Dublin in 1763, Theobald Wolfe Tone felt more strongly about being Irish than being Protestant. His efforts to free Ireland from Britain's control ended in defeat, but his message has long encouraged nationalists and has threatened loyalists.

Corbis-Bettmann

manufacturing plants turned flax grown on the Irish island into linen, and shipyards provided naval and merchant ships to Great Britain. Many Catholics came to the cities to look for work. They did not have the financial resources to begin their own businesses, so they often took jobs in Protestant-owned factories at low wages.

SOCIETY OF UNITED IRISHMEN

But Irish Catholics weren't off the playing field. Once again out of Ulster came a challenge to British rule—and this time the movement was led by a Protestant lawyer. In 1791 Theobald Wolfe Tone founded the Society of United Irishmen in Belfast. Wolfe Tone believed that people living on the Irish island, regardless of religion, had more in common with one another than any of them did with the British. Britain ran Ireland in Great Britain's interest, Wolfe Tone reasoned. "From my earliest youth," he said, "I have regarded the connection between Great Britain and Ireland as the curse of the Irish nation and felt convinced that whilst it lasted, this country could never be free or happy."

Wolfe Tone wanted to change people's thinking—

> *"From my earliest youth, I have regarded the connection between Great Britain and Ireland as the curse of the Irish nation and felt convinced that whilst it lasted, this country could never be free or happy."*
>
> Theobald Wolfe Tone

no longer should only Catholics be considered Irish and Protestants be considered British. The term "Irish" should refer to all people sharing the Irish island. According to Wolfe Tone, if all people living on the island united, the Irish could run Ireland on behalf of themselves. Challenging British rule wasn't far below the surface, but first, the United Irishmen concentrated on demanding that all Irish—regardless of religion—be legal equals. Because the laws in Ireland had mostly oppressed Catholics, this goal was usually referred to as Catholic **emancipation**.

To prevent an uprising, in 1793 the Irish Parliament under strong pressure from the British government passed the Catholic Relief Act. The act gave Catholics the right to obtain higher education, to vote, and to serve in many public offices but not in the British Parliament. Wolfe Tone pressed for more, and the United Irishmen came closer to advocating revolution.

Although Wolfe Tone and many of the United Irishmen were Protestants, he did not speak for all Protestants. Some of Ulster's wealthier and more powerful Protestants did not want to lose the financial and political advantages they enjoyed. These Protestants felt they would lose their privileged status if Catholics gained rights. Protestant peasants also feared for their safety. They remembered the thousands

of Protestant planters slaughtered before Cromwell suppressed the Catholic uprising of the 1640s. As a result, a group of Protestants formed the Orange Order, a group that included a paramilitary arm.

Meanwhile, British authorities cracked down on the United Irishmen, and Wolfe Tone supported outright rebellion. In 1796 Wolfe Tone arranged for France—which was spreading its own revolution against a monarch—to send ships and troops to help Ireland overthrow British rule. Stormy seas in Bantry Bay, at the southwestern tip of the island, hampered the landing of the French ships. Having lost the element of surprise, the French returned home.

Although the United Irishmen's planned attack at Bantry Bay didn't happen, the British realized how great a threat the group posed. In 1798 Wolfe Tone tried once more to stage a rebellion, again with French help. The British intercepted his landing party, captured Wolfe Tone, and put him on trial. In prison and sentenced to hang, Wolfe Tone committed suicide.

CHAPTER

3

ENTRENCHED POSITIONS

The British government responded to the Wolfe Tone Rebellion and the rest of the turmoil in Ireland with the Act of Union in 1801. The act officially joined Ireland and Great Britain. Instead of being Great Britain's nearest colony, Ireland became, at least technically, an integral portion of a new country—the United Kingdom of Great Britain and Ireland. (The term "unionist," which describes those in contemporary Northern Ireland who favor remaining part of the United Kingdom, dates from this act.)

Under the new legislation, Ireland's Parliament in Dublin disbanded, and Irish representatives took 100 seats in Britain's Parliament at Westminster Palace in London. The British Parliament consisted of two houses—the House of Commons and the House of Lords. Members of the House of Commons, elected by popular vote, often represented the interests of trade and urban areas. Members of the House of Lords, who were mostly wealthy landowners, inherited their seats. The House of Lords had the power to stop bills passed by the House of Commons from becoming laws.

British prime minister William Pitt, architect of the union, thought the act would make Ireland easier to control. He assumed that raising Ireland's legal status would enhance Irish loyalty to Britain. Pitt promised that full political emancipation for Catholics would soon follow, so Catholics at first favored the union. Full emancipation meant that Catholics would be able to serve in the House of Commons. This political right had been refused to Catholics under the Catholic Relief Act, which the Irish Parliament had passed almost a decade earlier. But King George III wouldn't allow Pitt to fulfill that promise, and Pitt resigned over the issue.

NATIONALIST MOVEMENT

Daniel O'Connell, a Catholic lawyer and spellbinding speaker from Dublin, became the leader of the drive for full Catholic emancipation. In 1828, although he was legally barred from serving in Parliament, O'Connell ran for a seat in the House of Commons and won. In 1829 the British government relented—fearing a new Irish rebellion might erupt—and pushed through the Roman Catholic Emancipation Act, which granted full legal equality to Catholics.

Able to take his seat at Westminster, O'Connell

made repeal of the Act of Union his top priority. Although the Roman Catholic Emancipation Act gave Catholics full political rights, in the Protestant-dominated British Parliament, Catholics were the minority. From O'Connell's viewpoint, for Irish Catholics to achieve freedom and equal rights in practice as well as in law, Ireland must become a sovereign nation. In a self-governed Ireland, Catholics would be the majority. (O'Connell and others in Ireland who favored discontinuing the union with Great Britain came to be called nationalists.)

The failure of O'Connell and other nationalists to obtain repeal of the Act of Union through peaceful, political means gave rise to more radical, revolutionary programs, notably the "Young Ireland" movement that flourished in the 1840s. Nothing, however, did more to radicalize the Irish than the ordeal that was to come.

THE POTATO FAMINE

In the 1800s, potatoes were the primary source of nutrition for most Irish except the wealthy classes. In fact, the poorest one-third of the population virtually survived on potatoes. A fungal blight, formerly unknown to the

Independent Picture Service

A woman and her children scrape the soil to find the last few potatoes. During the potato famine of the 1840s, a fungus ruined the island's staple crop, causing widespread starvation and disease.

Millions of Irish people emigrated to escape the potato famine. Many started new lives in the United States but never forgot their homeland.

British Isles, caused the total failure of the Irish potato crop in 1845 and 1846. For each of the next five years, Ireland suffered partial crop failures.

Estimates of the number of people in Ireland who starved to death range from about one million to almost two million. To escape the famine, another two million Irish immigrated to the United States (and 750,000 moved to Britain) between 1845 and 1855. Once begun, the emigration from Ireland continued even after the famine had subsided. By 1900 more than four million people had left Ireland for the United States.

Throughout the famine, even though millions of people on the island were starving, landlords of large Irish estates exported to Britain food crops that weren't affected by the blight. The British government did send some relief supplies, but the measures were universally viewed as too little, too late.

Even so, some British were afraid that the aid they did send to Ireland would create an unhealthy reliance on government handouts, and they pushed for cutting off the supplies.

Although no portion of Ireland was spared the effects of the famine, Ulster suffered the least because it was the island's most industrialized region. Nevertheless, 20 to 25 percent of Ulster's population died or emigrated.

In the mid-nineteenth century, Ulster's linen manufacturing and shipbuilding industries were thriving. The predominantly Protestant population that managed and worked in those industries earned a living independent of farming. But the many Catholics who worked in low-paying urban jobs could not afford to pay the high price for imported food. Lacking manufacturing industries, western Ireland—populated almost entirely by Catholics—was hit hardest by the famine.

INDEPENDENCE MOVEMENTS

As a result of the potato famine, hatred of Irish people for the British government increased. The lack of adequate aid while millions starved reinforced the long-held belief that the British viewed Irish Catholics as subhuman. The hatred spread to the Irish neighbor-

New textile looms boosted Belfast's linen-making industry in the early and mid-1800s. Most of the factory managers were Protestant; many of the low-paid workers were Catholic.

hoods of America. (In fact, Irish-Catholic and Irish-American lore sometimes portrays the great famine as a deliberate British policy to reduce the Catholic population in Ireland through starvation and emigration.)

By no coincidence, the decades just after the famine gave birth to new and radical movements for Irish independence. For example, the Irish Republican Brotherhood (IRB), whose members came to be known as republicans, was founded. The IRB had a revolutionary agenda and a willingness to use violence to achieve freedom from Britain. Irish Americans organized a secret society known as the Fenian Brotherhood. (The word *Fenian* referred to a legendary band of ancient Gaelic warriors.) The Fenians' aim was to overthrow British rule in Ireland, and they formed connections with the IRB, sending the organization money and supplies.

The Catholic Church opposed the IRB and any other organization that advocated violent tactics. Most of those who wanted less British involvement in Ireland's affairs were committed to peaceful, parliamentary means to advance their cause. In the late nineteenth and early twentieth centuries, the great cry was for Home Rule. This meant that Ireland would remain under British control in matters such as foreign and defense policy but that a relatively independent Irish Parliament would set Irish domestic policies.

In the mid-1870s, Charles Stewart Parnell—an Irish member of the British Parliament—emerged as the greatest advocate of the Home Rule campaign. Parnell's popularity stemmed from the support he got from the Catholic majority, although Parnell himself was Protestant. Because Home Rule would increase Catholics' say in the politics of the Irish island, the majority of Catholics favored the policy, whereas most Ulster Protestants opposed it. According to one Ulsterite slogan: *Home Rule would mean Rome Rule.* In other words, many Protestants in Ireland feared political domination by Catholics, who, these Protestants believed, would take their orders from the pope in Rome. In 1893, not long after Parnell's death, a Home Rule Bill did pass in the House of Commons but the House of Lords blocked its passage.

Portraits of those who worked to win Irish Home Rule surround a Fenian banner. At the bottom is Daniel O'Connell, known in Irish history as the "Great Emancipator."

North Wind Picture Archives

In the late nineteenth century, the drive toward Home Rule was gaining momentum. In Ulster, however, most Protestants were decidedly against the movement. Here, police officers enter the Shankill Road area of Belfast— then as now a Protestant section—to quiet a Home Rule protest that had turned violent.

In 1912 the House of Commons again approved a Home Rule Bill, but the Lords again rejected it. Under a new parliamentary procedure, however, the Lords couldn't delay passage of a bill for longer than two years if the House of Commons continued to pass it. It seemed Home Rule for Ireland had acquired unstoppable momentum.

If defeating Home Rule wasn't possible, Ulster loyalists pressed to exclude the northern portion of the island from the policy. They threatened to rise up if Britain abandoned them to the rule of the island's Catholic majority. To organize their protest against Home Rule, some Protestant loyalists set up the Ulster Volunteer Force, a paramili-

tary group. When the members of the UVF drilled in the streets of Ulster, British military officials showed tolerance bordering on sympathy. When illegal arms arrived for the UVF, the authorities allowed the shipments to land.

A Home Rule Bill passed in the House of Commons for a third time in 1913 and was vetoed again by the

House of Lords. The UVF stepped up its threatening words and actions, vowing never to submit peacefully to Home Rule. In March 1914, 57 British cavalry officers announced they would resign rather than force Ulster to accept Catholic rule. Nor did they want to be responsible for controlling the Protestant paramilitary. Most members of the House of Commons still favored Home Rule for the whole island, and under the new parliamentary procedures the House of Lords couldn't stop the bill from becoming law.

Britain was busy with other pressing concerns. At the same time as the Irish Home Rule question heated up, World War I (1914–1918) loomed. To resolve the issue in Ireland, King George V urged that the Protestant-dominated counties be excluded from the Home Rule plan. Parliament gave in. Legislators finally passed the Home Rule Bill in 1914, with a provision that six of the nine counties of Ulster could opt to remain part of the United Kingdom. Six weeks later, Britain declared war on Germany. Implementation of Home Rule was postponed.

THE EASTER RISING

To some moderate Irish, who had set aside their mistrust of the British to work by parliamentary means, passage of the Home Rule Bill suggested that Ireland could attain justice without violence. Other Irish, including the IRB, didn't believe justice under British rule was possible and weren't prepared to settle for Home Rule. They wanted independence, and to get it they were willing to make common cause with Germany, Britain's chief enemy in World War I.

The Home Rule Bill, which excluded six of the nine counties in Ulster, passed in 1914. Implementation was delayed by the outbreak of World War I (1914–1918). Posters showed the women of Ulster in support of Britain's effort to defeat the Germans.

Dublin's Sackville Street, which had hosted a rousing demonstration in support of Home Rule in 1912 (above), was badly damaged in the Easter Rising of 1916 (below). The Irish Republican Brotherhood (IRB), a group that sought complete independence from Britain, organized the rebellion.

In the middle of the global conflict, the IRB sought help from Germany to overthrow British rule in Ireland. Germany sent arms, but the British intercepted the ship. Meanwhile, in Dublin, rebels went forward with the planned revolt on Easter Monday of 1916. Called the Easter Rising, the rebellion was partially successful. The IRB occupied several government buildings, raised a flag over the post office (which became rebel headquarters), and declared an Irish republic. The rebels failed, however, to capture Dublin Castle, the well-fortified seat of British rule in Ireland, nor did they inspire a mass uprising. Five days and more than 1,000 casualties later, the rebels surrendered. The British executed 15 leaders of the rebellion.

At first, Irish public opinion had solidly opposed the uprising. With thousands of Irish troops in British uniform fighting against Germany, the time for conspiring with Germany seemed wrong. But the spectacle of British authorities condemning and executing IRB leaders swayed public opinion. A relatively new political party

Left: *After the Easter Rising, British troops escorted an IRB member to prison.* Right: *American-born Eamon de Valera escaped execution because he still held U.S. citizenship, although he'd lived in Ireland since childhood. Head of Sinn Féin, the political party that openly called for Irish self-rule, de Valera became the first president of the independent Irish state in 1919.*

called Sinn Féin benefited primarily from the shift in public sentiment.

WAR FOR INDEPENDENCE

Meaning "We Ourselves," Sinn Féin was the only legal political party that advocated an independent Irish republic. Support for the party swelled dramatically after the Easter Rising. In 1918 Sinn Féin won a majority of the Irish seats in the British Parliament. Because Sinn Féin pushed for separation from Britain, none of the party members took their seats in the House of Commons.

Instead, in 1919, Sinn Féin established a separate parliament in Dublin, calling the body the Dáil Éireann (Gaelic for the Assembly of Ireland), and declared Irish independence. The newly declared republic came ready-made with a constitution and an elected president, the Sinn Féin leader Eamon de Valera.

Britain sent troops to suppress the Dáil and to reestablish control over Ireland. The self-declared independent country defended itself with soldiers from the Irish Republican Army (IRA), Sinn Féin's military arm. Fighting without uniforms and gaining renown for its **guerrilla** tactics, the IRA forced the fighting into unconventional modes. From 1919 to 1921, as the line blurred between official combatants and civilians, Ireland became embroiled in a brutal war.

The Dáil claimed all of Ireland as the new republic's territory. Ulster's Protestants threatened to **secede** from Ireland if Ireland withdrew from the United Kingdom. While the war raged, the British Parliament offered a compromise. Under the Government of Ireland Act of 1920, two separate states would be created. Each would have its own local parliament and would remain under the loose control of the British Parliament in London.

DIVIDING IRELAND

Protestants in the north immediately agreed to the British proposal. Because Protestants dominated much of Ulster, the same six counties that had been granted exclusion from Home Rule ratified the Government of Ireland Act in May of 1921. After this time, the northeastern section of the Irish island officially became Northern Ireland, a province of the United Kingdom. The United Kingdom became the United Kingdom of Great Britain and Northern Ireland.

Under this new arrangement, Northern Ireland would send representatives to the British Parliament, which would control matters such as defense and taxation. But Northern Ireland would establish its own parliament to handle the province's domestic matters. The new province's government also would include a governor as well as a prime minister and a cabinet.

Later that year, the Anglo-Irish treaty—an arrangement hammered out between the British and some of the Dáil's leaders—came before

Opposed by Britain, the new Irish nation formed the Irish Republican Army (IRA), which often used guerrilla tactics to fight British troops. Here, soldiers examine a trench dug by IRA members during an ambush.

Imperial War Museum

CHAPTER

4

THE PRESENT CONFLICT

Since the division of Ireland in 1920, the IRA hadn't given up its goal to unite the island at any cost. In the mid-1950s, the IRA—in an attempt to reintegrate the island—launched a campaign of bombings and shootings in Northern Ireland that was designed to drive out the British. Primary targets were public places—such as restaurants and pubs—where British soldiers and RUC officers gathered. The IRA also attacked trucks loaded with British soldiers or government supplies. Receiving no official government support from the Republic and little popular backing among northern Catholics, the campaign failed, and the IRA abandoned it in 1962.

Economics may have played a role in the response of Northern Ireland's Catholics, who represented a disproportionately high share of the poor and the unemployed. Northern Ireland was enjoying the benefits of the United Kingdom's growing welfare state. As one of the poorest areas of the United Kingdom, Northern Ireland and its Catholic population received funds from social programs and saw their standard of living improve.

Into this situation came Terence O'Neill, a Protestant and leader of the Unionist Party, who'd become Northern Ireland's prime minister in 1963. Although the Unionist Party traditionally looked after Protestant interests, one of O'Neill's goals was to close the cultural and economic gap between Catholics and Protestants. He supported programs to create new housing for both Catholics and Protestants. Because living conditions of Catholics were often worse than those of Protestants,

many benefits from O'Neill's social programs funneled into the Catholic community. O'Neill also wanted to expand Northern Ireland's industries to create new jobs.

Meanwhile, the Reverend Ian Paisley, a minister of the Free Presbyterian Church, started a movement to block O'Neill's efforts. Paisley wanted the line between Protestants and Catholics to remain clearly defined.

By the late 1940s, Éire had renamed itself the Republic of Ireland, and the people of the United Kingdom of Great Britain and Northern Ireland were enjoying the benefits of a variety of state-funded welfare programs.

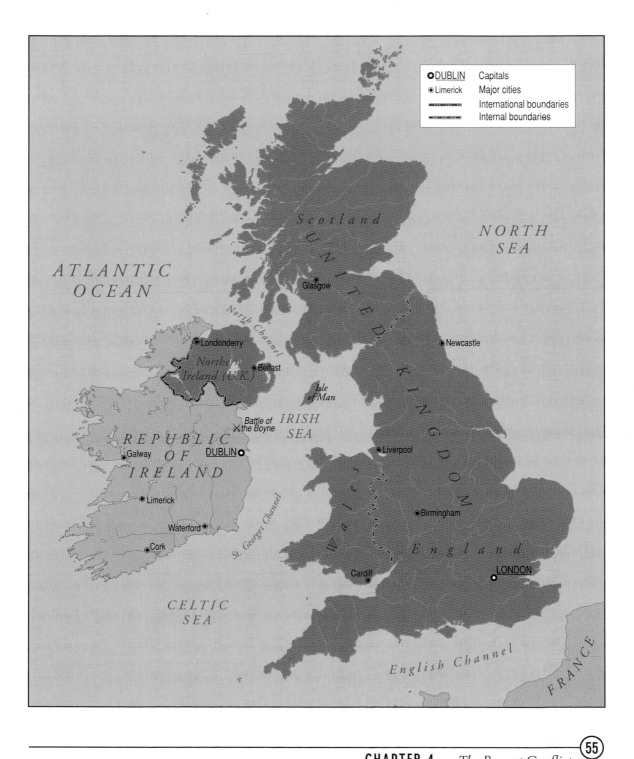

ATLANTIC
OCEAN

NORTH
SEA

Scotland

UNITED

●Glasgow

●Newcastle

North Channel

●Londonderry

Northern
Ireland (U.K.)

●Belfast

Isle
of Man

IRISH
SEA

Battle of
the Boyne

REPUBLIC

●Galway

OF

IRELAND

DUBLIN ●

●Liverpool

KINGDOM

Wales

●Birmingham

St. Georges Channel

England

●Limerick

●Waterford

●Cork

CELTIC
SEA

Cardiff ●

LONDON ●

English Channel

FRANCE

○DUBLIN   Capitals
●Limerick   Major cities
━━━━━━   International boundaries
━━━━━━   Internal boundaries

Paisley made impassioned speeches that drew support from a radical element of the Protestant community. This group feared that any concessions made to improve the living conditions of Catholics in Northern Ireland would take away the privileges to which Protestants were accustomed. Tensions between Protestants and Catholics began to mount. Protestant paramilitary groups, including the Ulster Volunteer Force—taking the name from the UVF formed in 1912—sprang up in the 1960s and quickly gained members.

PEACE MARCHES AND RIOTS

The economic benefits of being part of the United Kingdom didn't outweigh Catholics' anger at discriminatory measures enacted by Protestant politicians. As the majority in Ulster, Protestants were able to control local politics as well as Northern Ireland's Parliament. Although Catholics were the majority in some cities, such as Londonderry, Protestant politicians were able to dismantle Catholic attempts to gain political power. For example, by

© Ed Kashi

Ian Paisley

In 1963 Ian Paisley, a Presbyterian minister without previous involvement in politics, organized a protest march when Belfast city hall lowered the British flag to mark the death of Pope John XXIII. Local authorities banned the march and fined Paisley when he went ahead with the demonstration. Paisley quickly became the main spokesperson for the most anti-Catholic, fiercely loyalist element of Northern Ireland's Protestant community. Leader of the DUP since its founding in the early 1970s, Paisley opposes any move toward changing Northern Ireland's constitutional status.

Paisley's stand has not changed since the 1960s, when he rallied support from mostly working-class Protestants against Catholic peace marchers. He viewed Prime Minister Terence O'Neill's social reforms as the beginning of a process that would strip Protestants of what they considered their rightful privileges.

In 1985 he objected to the Anglo-Irish Agreement, which granted the Republic a say in how Northern Ireland is run. He harshly criticizes Britain, whom he fears will allow the Republic and the PIRA to chase the British out of the province. In the early 1990s, during the 17-month cease-fire, Paisley was insistent that Sinn Féin not be included in peace talks because the PIRA was still armed and had not declared a permanent truce.

Paisley hasn't confined his wrath to the Catholics and the British. During the mid-1990s, Paisley criticized James Molyneaux then leader of the Ulster Unionist Party, Northern Ireland's largest political party, for not resisting initiatives that demanded unionist concessions. Paisley vowed he wouldn't work with Molyneaux to develop a united Protestant position until Molyneaux repented.

In 1968 students marched from Belfast University to the city hall carrying banners in favor of civil rights and better housing for Northern Ireland's Catholics.

drawing district boundaries in ways that reduced the number of Catholics in a district—a tactic known as gerrymandering—the political elite guaranteed a Protestant majority on district councils even in cities where Catholics made up most of the population. In matters that affected day-to-day life, such as housing, hiring, and law enforcement practices, Protestant councils discriminated against Catholics. The RUC was almost entirely Protestant. In spite of O'Neill's efforts, housing rules gave preference to Protestants when assigning public housing.

In 1967, inspired by the U.S. Civil Rights movement led by Martin Luther King Jr., a group of middle-class Catholics in Belfast formed the Northern Ireland Civil Rights Association (NICRA) to protest discrimination. The group organized peaceful marches. NICRA's avowed goal was to achieve equality for Catholics within Northern Ireland, not unification with the Republic. Yet some Protestant extremists didn't believe NICRA's leaders. These extremists thought NICRA's tactics were a disguised attempt to resurrect the earlier IRA campaign to reunite Ireland by force.

Protestant paramilitaries, such as the UVF, reacted to NICRA protests with violence. In August of 1968, NICRA led between 2,500 and 4,000 people on a march from Coalisland to Dungannon. Marchers gathered in response to the following housing decision: an unmarried Protestant girl in the Dungannon Council area had received new government-funded housing, while there was a long list of large Catholic families in crowded conditions in need of housing. (Often a two-bedroom home housed as many as 15 to 20 people, perhaps two to three Catholic families.) This march ended peacefully, although Protestant extremists organized a counterdemonstration that interrupted

NICRA's route into Dungannon's town center.

When NICRA announced an October march through Londonderry, the government tried to ban it. But NICRA went ahead with the march. Baton-wielding RUC officers, in full view of international television cameras, attacked the marchers.

Meanwhile, in the face of official and paramilitary attacks, Catholics who advocated peaceful protest began to lose influence to nationalists who said force was the only language the other side could understand. A splinter branch of the IRA, calling itself the Provisional IRA (or PIRA), emerged in 1969. This group, even more radical than the original IRA, offered to protect Catholics from Protestant violence. The Provisionals took up the guerrilla war to end British rule and unify Ireland. The previous IRA—which came to be called the Official IRA to distinguish it from the Provisionals—faded from the scene.

In January 1969, more violence erupted between Catholic peace marchers and Protestant loyalist extremists. The People's Democracy—a group of university students who viewed Northern Ireland's conflict as hav-

Civil rights activists, police, and loyalist extremists clashed on January 4, 1969, on a road southeast of Londonderry. A peace march triggered the confrontation and rioting spread to Catholic neighborhoods. Many observers date "the troubles," the name often given to the conflict in Northern Ireland, from this time.

ing purely economic rather than ethnic roots—organized a 73-mile march from Belfast to Londonderry. After setting off on New Year's Day, the marchers encountered loyalist groups who threw stones or attacked with clubs.

Then, on January 4, on a bridge just a few miles from Londonderry, the loyalist extremists beat the marchers with planks, bottles, and metal pipes and threw some protesters off the bridge into the Burntollet River. RUC officers stood nearby without taking action to stop the attack. Members of the Ulster Special Constabulary—a part-time, all-Protestant police force also known as the B Specials—actively participated in beating the marchers.

Catholics in nearby Londonderry reacted to the Burntollet Bridge incident with rioting that lasted much of the night. In response, the RUC invaded Bogside, a Catholic district and PIRA stronghold, attacking residents and damaging their homes.

Rioting broke out in Belfast in August 1969. A rumor had started that Catholics had attacked

Bernadette Devlin McAliskey

In 1968, while attending Queen's University in Belfast, Bernadette Devlin became one of the founders of the People's Democracy, a student civil rights movement. In January 1969, she helped orchestrate the movement's march from Belfast to Londonderry. Violence between marchers and loyalist extremists—whose force was boosted by the B Specials—broke out during the march. Devlin was later to comment, "In retrospect, I realized the police had actually done us a great favor. . . .The civil rights movement had started out as a small middle-class pressure group, but it took only one day of police violence to transform it into a mass movement."

In 1969 her popularity as a civil rights leader—as well as the backing of local nationalist leaders—won Devlin a seat in Britain's House of Commons. The youngest woman ever to be elected to Parliament, she railed against the unionist-dominated government in Northern Ireland in her first speech.

By the mid-1970s, Devlin had married Michael McAliskey and had started a family. Her activism continues, focusing on prisoners' rights, Catholic unemployment, and the reunification of Ireland. She pays special attention to the rights of Irish women, whom she says, "are not only leading the political fight; they also hold the families together."

Independent Picture Service

marchers in a loyalist parade. Days of violence began at the boundary between a Catholic and Protestant neighborhood and spread to other parts of the city. Protestants from the Shankill Road area entered the mostly Catholic Unity Walk flats and began setting houses on fire with gasoline bombs. In this incident, the RUC tried hard to protect the Unity Walk Catholics from harm.

What's in a Name?

Officially called Londonderry, Northern Ireland's second largest city is also known to many people as Derry. In fact, the city council—when it achieved a nationalist majority—changed its name to Derry City Council. Return addresses on mail leaving the city bear either name. The name used reveals a great deal more than geographical location about the person sending the piece of mail. Most likely if an envelope is being sent from Derry, the person mailing it is Catholic. If the mail is sent from Londonderry, the individual is almost always Protestant.

By covering up the "London" part of this county sign, a Catholic has indicated a preference for the historic name of the county and city.

Derry was the original Irish name for the city. In 1613 the English added the prefix "London" in recognition of the financial help London merchants provided in the plantation of Ulster. For centuries the city had a Protestant majority, and Catholics were not allowed to live within its limits, although they could settle outside the city walls and across the river.

In 1689 the Catholic king James II, attempting to take back the throne he had lost to the Protestant king William of Orange, led an army to Londonderry. The Protestant Apprentice Boys bolted Londonderry's gates to keep out the troops. King James's army besieged the city for 105 days. James's forces finally retreated, but thousands of Protestants had died of starvation.

With the industrial revolution, the number of Catholics in the city grew. Eventually, in 1881, Londonderry acquired a Catholic majority. Many Catholics think the city should be known by Derry, its original Irish name. From their viewpoint, the name Londonderry symbolizes Protestant dominance. Protestants who feel strongly linked to Britain and feel strongly about honoring those who died defending the city maintain that Londonderry is the proper name. Changing the name would be like admitting defeat to the Catholics their ancestors had held off 300 years ago. Like so much else in Northern Ireland, the name of one of the province's largest cities—and counties—remains a source of conflict.

The Marching Season

Every summer a tradition known as the "marching season" inflames the hatred between the two ethnic-religious communities of Northern Ireland. During the season, thousands of parades take place throughout the province. The marchers commemorate the victories of their ancestors in the centuries-old conflict between Protestants and Catholics and between British loyalists and Irish nationalists.

Protestant civic groups, such as the Apprentice Boys, the Royal Black Institution, and the Orange Order, participate in more than 2,500 parades. Catholic organizations hold many marches in the spring to observe the anniversary of the Easter Rising of 1916. The routes of most of the parades don't enter the other ethnic-religious community's neighborhoods, so most marches don't trigger violent confrontations.

The biggest and most inflammatory marches occur in July, when Protestants celebrate the victory in 1690 of William of Orange over the troops of the Catholic king James II in the Battle of the Boyne. Marchers don the traditional costume of black suit, orange sash, and bowler hat. Some Protestant marchers use the parades as an opportunity to taunt the Catholic community, reminding them of the privileged position Protestants have held in Northern Ireland's society. By chanting anti-Catholic slogans and singing sacrilegious songs about the pope, rowdier elements insult Catholics, who often take the bait, and riots break out.

In recent years, the RUC has tried to prevent the annual confrontation between Protestant marchers and Catholic protesters. But any remedy has been viewed as favoring one group or the other. When the RUC has banned the Orange Order from going through Catholic neighborhoods, Protestants have rioted. When the RUC has allowed the parades to proceed, Catholics have revolted. Preventing violence during the marching season seems to be in the hands of Northern Ireland's citizens.

Loyalists of Portadown wear traditional clothing during the July commemoration of the Battle of the Boyne.

BRITISH TROOPS ARRIVE

Two more riots erupted in August of 1969. In Londonderry on August 12, Catholics threw stones at participants in the Apprentice Boys' March—an annual gathering that celebrates the anniversary of the young Protestant apprentices who in 1689 shut the heavy gates of Londonderry to keep out the Catholic king James II. The RUC and those who supported the Apprentice Boys' March stormed Bogside. Loyalist vigilantes—to show Catholics they had no safe refuge—terrorized the neighborhood.

Violence mounted quickly, and both sides hurled bricks and gasoline bombs. Bogsiders soon sealed off all roads into the neighborhood and announced that no Protestants would be admitted to the district—a "No Go" area, in the jargon of Northern Ireland.

The RUC tried to contain Bogsiders, whom they feared would attempt to attack Protestant areas of Londonderry. Open warfare broke out between the Catholic residents and the mostly Protestant police force. On the third day of fighting, in what came to be called the Battle of Bogside, the British army stepped in—marking the British troops' first involvement in Northern Ireland's recent conflict.

During the night of August 14, as rioting quieted in Londonderry, violence broke out in Belfast's Falls Road neighborhood, another Catholic district. The RUC, the B Specials, and Protestant extremists rampaged through the streets. Mem-

Left: *In August 1969, a pair of British soldiers kept watch on Belfast after rioting had caused widespread destruction and injury.* Facing page: *Another soldier stands amid the rubble of burned-out buildings and the gutted hulks of vehicles.*

UPI/Corbis-Bettmann

bers of these various military and paramilitary groups burned many Catholic homes. In the ensuing gunfire, eight people were killed and hundreds were injured. The excessive force used by the RUC further fueled Catholic distrust.

Britain sent more troops to Northern Ireland to control the violence in Belfast and to act as peacekeepers. Given the historic attitudes toward Britain, observers of the conflict were surprised to note that Catholics welcomed the troops and that Protestants resented their arrival. Britain assumed command of security in Northern Ireland, which had previously been controlled by Northern Ireland's Protestant-dominated organizations. Some Protestants felt betrayed that the British had taken away their authority. But the violence during the previous months had demonstrated that the local police weren't neutral in the war that was breaking out.

Until the British army arrived, Catholics had had no one but illegal paramilitaries to protect them. Because the British army seemed committed to even-handed peacekeeping, Catholics felt they had a legitimate authority monitoring their security. By mid-1970, Britain had sent many thousands of troops to bring peace and to win the "minds and hearts" of the local people. On the doorsteps of Catholic communities, residents served tea to soldiers. In discos young women danced with British soldiers. In the streets, children played games with members of the troops. Protestants keenly felt their loss of power in running the province.

BRITAIN'S REPUTATION

During 1970 and 1971, Catholic opinion toward the British troops began to shift. The PIRA, which defined Britain as the source of Ireland's problems, portrayed the troops as members of an army of occupation. In a **propaganda** campaign to turn Catholics away from the British and toward the PIRA, the paramilitary group exaggerated some of the blunders

to help the Protestants get the Catholics under control. The propaganda campaign worked, and British response to attacks encouraged more Catholics to back the PIRA.

In this charged atmosphere, the people of Northern Ireland formed three new political parties—the Social Democratic and Labour Party, the Alliance Party (AP), and the Democratic Unionist Party. The slo-

of mostly middle-class voters from both the Catholic and the Protestant communities. The DUP, headed by Ian Paisley, drew mostly working-class Protestants who strongly objected to giving in to Catholic demands for social change and to any move toward cutting ties with Britain.

In 1971 Britain gave the security forces in Northern Ireland special internment powers to arrest and jail suspected terrorists without filing charges and without respect for other citizen rights. Many Catholics saw internment as evidence that the British government and the Protestant militants of Northern Ireland were allied against them. The security forces applied this special power almost exclusively to members of the Catholic community. As a result of internment, support for the PIRA increased dramatically among Catholics in Northern Ireland.

The low point for Britain's effort to appear even-handed occurred on Sunday, January 30, 1972. Londonderry Catholics, defying a British ban on all demonstrations, staged a march to protest the intern-

> *"That was 1969. That was the goodness of Northern Ireland. Then it was simply Catholic versus Protestant and vice versa. There was no one there to say, 'Right, let's get the "Brits" out!' It was great. Then we were the Catholics' saviours. We were there to help them and not the Protestants. Then slowly but surely we went full circle. Now we're the pig in the middle and everybody hates us."*
>
> British army corporal

committed by British soldiers. Terrorist attacks changed the way in which the British soldiers responded to the Catholic community, too. The more the British tried to crack down on attacks committed by the PIRA, the more the troops reinforced the impression that they had come

gan of the SDLP was "Civil Rights for All and Just Distribution of Wealth." This party attracted primarily Catholics who advocated social and economic change brought about through nonviolent means. The moderate AP, which attempted to bridge the religious divide, appealed to a small number

Above: *In Londonderry, during violence that erupted on January 30, 1972, British troops rounded up Catholic marchers who had been demonstrating in defiance of a ban. The violence left 13 people dead.*
Below: *A few days later, mourners filed past the closed coffins of some of the victims, whose deaths the PIRA vowed to avenge.*

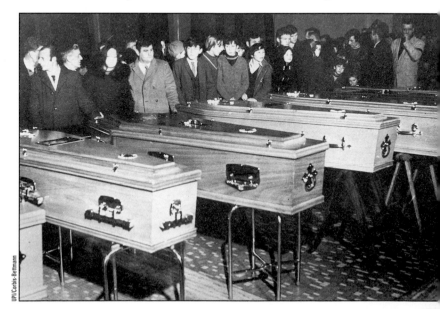

ment policy. British troops confronted the marchers. It's not clear what started the violence—each side would later claim the other fired first—but the troops shot into a mob of mostly unarmed protesters, killing 13 people and injuring many others.

In the weeks following this event, which has become known as Bloody Sunday, violence escalated. Terrorist acts numbered in the hundreds. On March 24, 1972, Britain's prime minister, Edward Heath, lost confidence that the Northern Ireland government could restore order and disbanded it. He instituted direct rule

The Community of the Peace People

In West Belfast in August 1976, a PIRA squadron tried to crash through a British army roadblock. The car swerved and crushed Anne Maguire, a young Catholic woman, and her four children. Only Maguire and one child survived. The incident, which touched a nerve among Northern Ireland's people, launched a movement.

Betty Williams, who lived in the neighborhood where the accident occurred, circulated a petition denouncing the PIRA for its role in perpetuating the violence. She collected 5,000 signatures in one afternoon. While Maguire recovered in the hospital, her sister, Mairead Corrigan, joined forces with Williams. Together they began the Community of the Peace People. Williams and Corrigan organized a series of peace marches and mass meetings that were well attended by men but were dominated by women. Donations from around the world poured in. In 1976 the two young women were awarded the Nobel Peace Prize.

The Peace People gave ordinary Catholics and Protestants in Northern Ireland a way to publicly express their desire for peace. Over the years, the group has shifted its focus from organizing mass demonstrations to quieter activities, such as helping former members of the paramilitary organizations make the transition to a life of nonviolence.

Betty Williams (left) *and Mairead Corrigan*

from London in what he hoped would be a short-term measure.

Because of policies like internment, as well as aggressive interrogation methods, Britain was judged guilty of torture in 1976 by the European Court of Human Rights and of inhuman treatment of prisoners in 1978. Britain's reputation continued to suffer from the army's actions and the government's policies. In the early 1980s, for example, international attention turned to Northern Ireland's Maze Prison, where dozens of PIRA members were held.

The PIRA wanted its members to be acknowledged as political prisoners whose crime was participation in the struggle to free Ireland from an army of occupation. To get this status, the inmates went on a hunger strike. They demanded they be given the privileges that political prisoners receive, such as exemption from prison work and the right to hold meetings among themselves. Perhaps the most publicized and the most symbolic demand the PIRA prisoners made was that they be allowed to wear

Left: *Masked PIRA members carry the coffin of Martin Hurson, who died in 1981 while on a hunger strike in Maze Prison. Nine other hunger-striking inmates—including Bobby Sands, who was elected to Parliament while in prison—eventually died.* Below: *Throughout the 1980s, the PIRA bombed sites in Britain and Northern Ireland. Harrod's, a large, fashionable department store in London, was hit in 1983.*

Oistin MacBride/Corbis-Bettmann

their own clothes. The British government refused. In the end, 10 of the hunger strikers died. The strikes finally ended when the families allowed the surviving strikers to be fed intravenously after they'd passed out from lack of food. The hunger strikes fueled a surge of support for Sinn Féin.

Throughout the 1980s, the PIRA stepped up its efforts through a campaign of bombings and assassinations in Northern Ireland, in Britain, and against British interests around the world. A PIRA

© Francis Diaz/Sygma

bomb exploded during the British Conservative Party's annual conference, killing several officials and narrowly missing Prime Minister Margaret Thatcher. Bombs in public places, such as in department stores, at tourist attractions, and at parades, were set off in Britain.

ANGLO-IRISH AGREEMENT

Late in 1985, Prime Minister Thatcher and Prime Minister Garret FitzGerald, from the Republic, signed an agreement they hoped would break the deadlock of violence. One of the agreement's measures was to set up the Intergovernmental Conference, through which British and Irish ministers would meet to discuss the affairs of Northern Ireland. This body had no specifically outlined powers, but its creation was symbolic. For the first time since the island had been split in 1920, Britain accepted as legitimate the Republic's interest in the affairs of Northern Ireland.

For its part, in another important first since the island's division, the Republic officially accepted the long-standing British position that Northern Ireland's status

The British and Irish governments took steps to stem the violence, resulting in the Anglo-Irish Agreement. Here, Irish prime minister Garret FitzGerald (left) and British prime minister Margaret Thatcher hold the signed document.

should not change without the agreement of the majority in the province. The Republic also agreed to cooperate more closely with Britain against terrorism.

Of the major political parties in Northern Ireland only the moderate SDLP praised the Anglo-Irish Agreement. Militant Catholics and militant Protestants followed their usual scenario. Sinn Féin—which saw the Republic's cooperation against ter-

rorism, especially PIRA activities, as the heart of the accord—rejected the Anglo-Irish Agreement. Unionist parties saw the agreement as a first step of the British plan to sell them out.

Ian Paisley and Harold McCusker (of the Democratic Unionist and Official Unionist Parties, respectively) joined forces and filed a letter of complaint that condemned the British action. "In the name of the

Unionist majority whose rights you have trampled in the gutter, we repudiate you. The sordid exercise in which you are involved is the very antithesis of democracy." Unionists organized demonstrations and mass rallies, some of which turned violent, to express opposition to the agreement and to the suggestion that the Republic should have anything to say about Northern Ireland.

LEADING TO A CEASE-FIRE

Between 1985 and 1992, the conference met and made limited progress toward a resolution. The unionist parties still balked at giving the Republic a say in discussions of Northern Ireland. They also demanded that the Republic put its constitution's claim of ultimate sovereignty over Northern Ireland before the Republic's electorate for a vote. The Republic refused.

During this period, the number of deaths attributed annually to the troubles dwindled, and it was more obvious than ever that the majority on each side wanted peace. Yet the paramilitaries who kept up the fighting hadn't really changed their views.

© Pacemaker Press International Ltd.

Although fewer casualties occurred, violence between Protestant and Catholic factions was still taking its toll in the late 1980s. Above: Police in Enniskillen cover up the bodies of victims of a PIRA bombing in 1987. Below: Members of a loyalist paramilitary fired at crowds gathered in 1988 at a cemetery where three PIRA guerrillas were being buried.

© B. Bisson/Sygma

Internment

For many years of the recent conflict, soldiers could arrest and imprison Northern Ireland citizens who were suspected of terrorism without charging them with a crime. Internment, as this antiterrorism policy was called, caused fury throughout the Catholic community when the British first implemented it in 1971.

International pressure played a large role in Britain's eventual decision to discontinue this policy in 1976. Some of those arrested under internment, however, were not released until the late 1980s. At that time, the British released several Irish Catholics against whom no evidence of terrorist activity had been found. Some had been imprisoned as long as 15 years.

Upon his release from prison in October 1989, Brian Conlon acknowledged well-wishers. Conlon had been interned in 1974 and wrongly convicted in 1975 of terrorist activities.

Developments between 1993 and 1996 made peace seem possible. In February 1993, the PIRA sent word that it might call off its violent campaign if it could participate in all-party talks to resolve Northern Ireland's problems. British official policy said Britain would never deal with the PIRA. Nevertheless, the British began to have regular secret contact with the PIRA. A British representative sent word that Sinn Féin could take part in such talks if the PIRA gave up violence.

In March 1993, the Republic reversed its previous position and expressed a willingness to amend its claim of sovereignty over the six counties of the north if it were part of an overall settlement on Northern Ireland. The Republic stated that constitutional changes proposed during peace talks would be put to a vote before its electorate.

Beginning in April 1993, John Hume, leader of the SDLP, and Gerry Adams, head of Sinn Féin, met secretly a number of times and

agreed on a common Catholic approach to the peace process. By participating in these discussions, each leader risked his political reputation and his life. The SDLP and Sinn Féin have always disagreed on whether violence to further political means is acceptable. To some supporters from each party, discussions between the leaders constituted betrayal.

In October 1993, British prime minister John Major and the Republic's prime minister, Albert Reynolds, committed their governments to a new drive for peace in Northern Ireland. Not until November 1993 did the British government publicly admit its reversal of policy in dealing with the PIRA. Up until this time, Britain had reassured the Protestants of Northern Ireland that the government would never negotiate with the PIRA. The news of the government's secret meetings with the PIRA escalated Protestant fears of being abandoned by Britain.

In spite of negative Protestant reaction to the all-party talks, plans for finding a solution to Northern Ireland's conflict continued. The highlight of these developments came in December 1993, when Britain and the Republic issued the Downing Street Declaration, setting out what they called a "framework for peace." The declaration pledged to support any arrangement, including Irish unification, that was acceptable to a majority of Northern Ireland's people. Prime Minister Major committed Britain to begin talks with Sinn Féin within three months of a permanent PIRA commitment to stop its campaign of violence.

John Hume

Since 1979 John Hume has led the SDLP, the political party supported by the majority of Northern Ireland's Catholics. Its philosophy reflects Hume's personal political beliefs, including equal pay for equal work, civil rights for all, proportional representation, and the eventual reunification of the Irish island with the consent of Northern Ireland's majority.

The party's goal of a united Ireland means that primarily Catholics vote for SDLP candidates. But Hume envisioned the party as a forum in which Northern Ireland's Catholic and Protestant voters could work together to make progress in areas of shared concern, such as the economy. When those advances are made, religion will cease to cause tension.

Hume views Northern Ireland's poor economy, which affects both Protestants and Catholics, as the province's underlying problem. Following this reasoning, terrorist violence will stop if the standard of living increases. At that point, when reconciliation has occurred between the two communities, Northern Ireland can be reintegrated into the Republic, a step Hume sees as necessary to ensure the island's future stability.

For many years, Hume, has been a member of the British House of Commons and has served in the European Parliament as well. While a member of these organizations, Hume has spread the issue of Northern Ireland's economy and has worked to bring foreign investment to the province.

During the early 1990s, Hume followed his firm belief that all voices must be heard if lasting peace is to be achieved. He secretly met with Sinn Féin leader Gerry Adams to establish a common Catholic approach to peace talks.

On August 31, 1994, the PIRA announced "a complete cessation of military operations." The united command of the Protestant paramilitary organization joined the cease-fire on October 13, 1994. This marked the first time since the recent conflict had begun that both sides had declared an open-ended cease-fire at the same time. On December 9, the British government met with Sinn Féin.

In February 1995, during the cease-fire, the British and Irish cabinets endorsed a "Framework for the Future" that contained ideas for bridging the disagreements between loyalists and nationalists. They suggested creating a new council with representatives from both Northern Ireland and the Republic's Parliament to coordinate policies north and south of the border.

Britain, which still maintained more than 15,000 troops in Northern Ireland, began withdrawing them a few hundred at a time. During 1995, Britain withdrew about 1,600 troops. In March 1995, the government announced that the remaining troops would no longer

In August 1994, fresh nationalist graffiti in Belfast expressed the desire for British troops to leave the province. Britain began withdrawing its forces soon afterward.

routinely patrol Belfast. For the first time in two decades, the streets of some Catholic neighborhoods in west Belfast were free of British troops.

Foreign governments, particularly the United States, nurtured the peace process. The cease-fire seemed to be lasting. Tourism and new investment rose, and unemployment dropped sharply. The end of the long conflict seemed to be in sight.

ROADBLOCKS TO PEACE

Despite the cease-fire and the apparent momentum of the peace process, there were obstacles on the horizon. Unionists deplored the ideas announced in the Anglo-Irish "Framework for the Future." They hated the idea of the cross-border council, which they saw as a step toward Britain's abandonment of their cause and Northern Ireland's eventual takeover by the Republic. Ian Paisley called the framework a "conspiracy" against northern Protestants. The DUP leader didn't want the British to talk to the PIRA or to Sinn Féin. Paisley didn't think it was enough for the PIRA to simply declare a cease-fire. He wanted the PIRA to apologize for all the chaos it had caused. Even the moderate Ulster Unionist Party was appalled. Party leader James Molyneaux said the Anglo-Irish document should be dropped as a basis for further negotiations. To address unionist concerns, the British government demanded that

President Clinton Encourages Peacemakers

During the 17-month cease-fire, the U.S. government tried to nurture the peace process in Northern Ireland. The emotional highlight of its efforts was President Bill Clinton's November 1995 trip to Belfast and Londonderry. In a speech before an audience of both Protestants and Catholics, Clinton—himself of Irish descent—urged Northern Ireland's citizens to keep pressing for peace. President Clinton delivered a powerful speech, but a nine-year-old Catholic girl named Catherine Hamill stole the show. Before a worldwide television audience, she read

Behind a bulletproof screen, U.S. president Bill Clinton addressed an enthusiastic crowd in front of Belfast's city hall.

aloud a letter to Clinton. "My first daddy died in the troubles. It was the saddest day of my life. . . . Now it is nice and peaceful. I like having peace and quiet for a change instead of people shooting and killing. My Christmas wish is that peace and love will last in Ireland forever."

Clinton's visit to Northern Ireland, the first ever by a U.S. president, boosted the province. The cease-fire seemed durable. Almost immediately the province saw how much better life might be if peace were established. Tourism reached record levels. New investments poured in. Unemployment fell sharply, and Northern Ireland's economy grew faster than that of the rest of the United Kingdom.

James Molyneaux

The province's more flamboyant politicians have upstaged James Molyneaux in the media. Yet he led Northern Ireland's largest political party—the Ulster Unionist Party—from 1979 through August 1995.

Once considered the lap dog of the British Conservative Party, the UUP under Molyneaux steered a more independent course. Especially in the early 1990s, when the Conservative prime minister John Major held a slim parliamentary majority, the UUP used its votes to help the Conservatives narrowly pass legislation. In return, the UUP expected Parliament's support on matters concerning Northern Ireland.

In February 1995, the prime ministers of Britain and the Republic of Ireland announced the "Framework for the Future." This document stated that Northern Ireland's constitutional status would not change without the consent of the province's majority. Fears of abandonment by Britain, however, led senior UUP officers to doubt not only the government's commitment to the framework's goals, but also Molyneaux's methods of leadership.

As a result, Molyneaux's rule of the UUP ended on a note of disappointment, but many supporters remember his accomplishments. He broadened the party's appeal by using political negotiations rather than violence to pressure Britain for its continued support. He criticized Paisley's approval of the loyalist paramilitary who, according to Molyneaux, did more damage to Northern Ireland than the PIRA did.

Molyneaux's departure from the UUP, which came during the 17-month cease-fire, leaves the direction of future peace talks more uncertain. David Trimble, who took over as UUP leader, has criticized the concessions, such as power sharing with the Republic, that the party made under Molyneaux. Many observers of the conflict wait anxiously to see what approach Trimble will take.

the PIRA disarm before Sinn Féin could be included in all-party talks. Meanwhile, Sinn Féin was becoming impatient and was beginning to doubt the sincerity of Britain's offer to negotiate.

On February 9, 1996, using secret codes, a PIRA spokesperson informed the Irish National Broadcast Authority that Britain had "squandered this unprecedented opportunity to resolve the conflict." An hour later, a huge explosion rocked a London business district known as the Docklands, killing two and sending dozens more to hospitals. The cease-fire was over.

A week later, police defused a bomb near London's theater district. Police said the bomb bore all the hallmarks of the PIRA. A few days later, the PIRA took responsibility for killing one person and injuring nine others when a bomb ripped apart a bus in London. Prime Minister Major vowed that the PIRA's resumption of hostilities would not end the peace process, but he also declared that the PIRA would not be allowed to "bomb their way to the negotiating table."

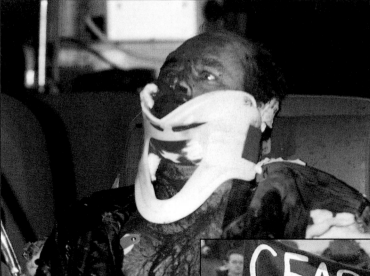

Left: *In February 1996, at a hospital in London, a man injured in a PIRA bus bombing was wheeled into the emergency room.* Below: *Although the bombings had ended the cease-fire, the people of Northern Ireland—Catholics and Protestants alike—gathered at rallies in favor of restarting the peace process.*

Express News/Archive Photos

© Alan Lewis/Sygma

Almost as soon as the PIRA cease-fire ended, a series of public demonstrations began. Demanding that the peace process go forward, 150,000 Catholic and Protestant citizens poured into the streets. A petition of 80,000 signatures insisted on an end to violence. Having had a taste of peace, the people of Northern Ireland were demanding that it last. 🌐

CHAPTER 5

WHAT'S BEING DONE TO SOLVE THE PROBLEM

The search for a peaceful solution to the conflict in Northern Ireland has tantalized and frustrated an entire generation. Government officials from Northern Ireland, from the Republic, from Britain, and from the United States—as well as international human rights groups, religious organizations, community groups, schools, families, and individuals—have participated in the attempt to find a remedy. To be fully successful, their answers must convince those who are resorting to violence to stop. So far, the shootings and bombings have continued.

The level of violence rises and falls with the tide of politics. Although it's clear all parties must agree, it is difficult to imagine that the conflict will end just by adopting a new official policy, no matter how brilliant the new policy may be. To be effective, change needs to come not only through legislation but through adjustments in people's attitudes of suspicion and hatred. Hundreds of years of history play into the view each group has of the other.

One consequence of the current conflict is that Northern Ireland's population is far more segregated than ever before. According to the 1991 census, only 7 percent lived in neighborhoods with both Catholic and Protestant residents. In a society where two groups have so little contact, bridges that give Protestants and Catholics reasons to interact are rare, and crossing them requires courage, especially in the face of the paramilitary groups that keep the conflict going. The solution that will end Northern Ireland's violence and enable its divided society to reintegrate must be acceptable to nationalist and loyalist paramilitary groups as well as to the governments of Britain and the Republic.

THE PROVISIONAL IRA

According to the PIRA, the presence of the British on the Irish island is the source of the problem. Withdrawal of British troops and the removal of all British influence is the solution. After the British leave Ireland alone, the PIRA insists, the primary cause of bad feelings between Catholics and Protestants will be removed.

Despite the violence, life goes on in Northern Ireland. Pushing strollers, two women cross a Belfast road bridge that is covered with security wire. The wire prevents extremists from dropping gas bombs and other small missiles on passing traffic.

People who are not from Northern Ireland find the degree of ethnic separation in the province difficult to comprehend. Tony Parker, a British journalist who lived in Belfast for several months in the early 1990s, relates a story from his early days in the city. When he dropped off film at a drugstore, the clerk asked him which of two film processors he preferred. At the time, Parker writes, he knew of no way to choose as he was unfamiliar with either company's quality of developing. Parker later realized that he had missed the clue—the clerk hadn't expected him to choose processors based on which would do the best work but to choose based on ethnicity. One processor had an Irish-Catholic name; the other a solidly Irish-Protestant name. The drugstore assumed that Catholics and Protestants wanted their film developed by a processor that shared their ethnic background.

© Bruce Haley

Young Catholics sun themselves beneath pro-PIRA graffiti. An illegal organization, the PIRA has about 400 active guerrilla fighters.

no longer find it worthwhile.

The PIRA does not acknowledge Northern Ireland as a legal entity. It claims the reason for such a province to exist is to justify Britain's illegal occupation of a portion of the Irish island. From the PIRA's perspective, anyone should be able to see from a glance at a map that the 6 counties called Northern Ireland are just as much a part of Ireland as the other 26.

The PIRA doesn't buy the argument that the northeastern portion of the island should be a separate political unit simply because the majority of people living there are Protestant. After all, the PIRA would respond, in the sixteenth century, Protestants were planted in Ireland, making the native Irish their subjects. To claim three centuries later that descendants of those Protestants are enti-

Yet because the PIRA believes Britain will never agree to depart peacefully, its unflinching mission is the violent campaign to drive out the British. The illegal paramilitary group intends to make the continued presence of the British so costly and unpleasant that Britain will

Imperial War Museum

The PIRA's historic commitment to violence as a way of forcing change has drawn in many Catholic teenagers.

tled to special consideration adds insult to injury. But they add that, after the British leave, Protestants who remain on the island and become Irish citizens will have nothing to fear about their treatment under the government of a united Ireland.

To the PIRA, Britain's condition that any change in Northern Ireland's status must be subject to the approval of the majority of the population of Northern Ireland is unjust. This condition makes the PIRA's goal of a united Ireland impossible as long as the Protestant majority of the north opposes it. Instead, the paramilitary group argues, the majority of the total population on the Irish island (that is, the Roman Catholic majority) should decide the question.

MILITANT PROTESTANTS

Militants within the Protestant community in Northern Ireland refuse to consider the unification of Ireland or any other formula that would require them to live under a Catholic-dominated government. They insist that Britain should not talk to Sinn Féin and certainly not to the PIRA itself about power-sharing or about a consultative process with the Republic. The militants fear that the Republic's influence could result in an unacceptable arrangement being forced upon them. Their anxiety is not unfounded, considering that the Republic's constitution has not yet been altered and still requires the eventual rejoining of the island's two parts.

Loyalists express great solidarity with Britain. They sometimes describe themselves as "more British than the British." Over the decades, they have grown fearful that their British allies will pull out of the costly, bloody, and increasingly unpopular task of occupying and subsidizing Northern Ireland. Protestants worry that when the economic and social strain of maintaining rule over Northern Ireland becomes too much, Britain will choose to let the province go. Although Britain states that it won't give in unless the majority in Northern Ireland wishes to be free of British rule, Protestants doubt Britain's sincerity.

Loyalists possess two principal means by which they can threaten Britain to con-

Militant Protestant groups have also attracted the young. Here, a boy holds the emblem of the Ulster Freedom Fighters (UFF)—a banned paramilitary organization associated with the UDA—before a parade down Belfast's Shankill Road.

Members of a UDA brigade posed in the capital in 1989, three years before the group was declared illegal.

tinue the alliance with Northern Ireland—voting and violence. Under the British governmental system, Loyalists control the majority of Northern Ireland's seats in the British Parliament and support the Conservative

> "We have a completely different culture [compared] to the Irish. . . . If I became Irish, I'd lose all my traditions. They're not going to come in and take over our country."

the prime minister must be from the party that holds a majority in Parliament. In most cases, the leader of the party that wins a majority becomes the prime minister. Parliamentary elections occur at least every five years.

Party (also known as the Tory Party). When the Conservative Party has only a slim majority, the Tory prime minister depends on the Northern Ireland Protestant vote. To get it, the Conservatives must reassure loyalists

that Britain will continue to uphold the loyalists' wishes for Northern Ireland.

The political power of Northern Ireland's loyalists loses a great deal of force when a Tory government has a large majority and does not need the loyalist vote. Loyalist votes also become less influential when the British Labour Party, which doesn't rely on the loyalists' support, has the majority. In these situations, Northern Ireland's loyalist extremists resort to the other means available to them. They threaten to initiate scenarios of horrific violence in Northern Ireland if

CHAPTER 5   *What's Being Done to Solve the Problem*

In May 1997, the Labour Party won a majority of seats in the British Parliament, and Tony Blair (above), *the party's leader, became prime minister. During a visit to Northern Ireland after taking power, Blair sounded impatient for the peace process to begin anew. Because most loyalists supported the rival Conservative Party, the Labour victory reduces loyalist parliamentary clout.*

Britain ever forces upon the Protestant majority an unacceptable arrangement. If the crisis ever reached that point, according to militant Protestants, Britain's choice would be between going to war against its own long-time allies or walking away from the situation in Northern Ireland. In so doing, the British would leave behind a bloodbath as Protestants take up arms against the island's Catholic majority.

THE BRITISH GOVERNMENT

The British government would like to withdraw its troops from Northern Ireland, to restore home rule, and to end all emergency security measures. The price of maintaining thousands of British troops in Northern Ireland has been high. In addition to the cost of security, the fact that Northern Ireland receives more from the national government in social spending than it pays in taxes has led many on the island of Great Britain to view control over Northern Ireland as more trouble and expense than it's worth. A final settlement that would lead to British withdrawal would be very popular in England, Scotland, and Wales. But the British government must weigh its desire to withdraw troops against its twin desire of fulfilling promises to Northern Ireland's Protestants and of not being defeated by terrorists.

New arrangements for Northern Ireland, including some form of mutual consultation or even power sharing with the Republic, will continue to be considered. Britain also has reiterated its willingness to relinquish rule over Northern Ireland if that ever becomes the expressed wish of the majority of Northern Ireland's citizens. Britain's flexibility stops short, however, when it is threatened by the PIRA. The PIRA, Britain maintains, will not succeed through terrorism within Northern Ireland or toward British citizens in other locations. As a result of its bombing tactics, the PIRA is widely hated in Britain. Officially, the British government has refused to negotiate with the PIRA until it announces an unconditional and permanent end to its violence.

REPUBLIC OF IRELAND

Among the conflict's many players, the Republic of Ireland is in the weakest position to assert pressure on the situation in Northern Ireland. The Irish constitution still pledges to work for political unification of the island. But in response to pressure from Northern Ireland's unionists, the Republic has agreed to put up for vote measures to amend its constitutional claim on Northern Ireland.

Immediately after the division of Ireland in 1920, many Catholics in the south felt strongly that an injustice had been committed. They claimed that the quest for Irish independence would remain incomplete until the entire island was under Irish rule. Over the decades, those feelings have weakened. In addition, the economic burden that would accompany the reunification of the Irish island causes concern among the Republic's citizens. Moreover, finding the

> *"Those that wish to see a united Ireland without coercion can argue for it. . . . If they succeeded, we would certainly respect that. But none of us . . . is likely to see Northern Ireland as anything but part of the United Kingdom."*
>
> Prime Minister Tony Blair

Although it remains to be seen what tack Prime Minister Blair will take in resolving the province's ongoing conflict, the government does want to remove its troops from Northern Ireland. Here, British soldiers fire at nationalist demonstrators in Londonderry.

Republic of Ireland's place in the European economy and even establishing better relations with Britain have become more pressing than uniting the island. Political parties, such as Sinn Féin, whose platforms make unification an urgent priority, receive only a small minority of the votes in the Republic. The major parties have adopted the view that unification is a noble goal but that it may not be practical.

WORKING FOR PEACE

In addition to cooperation from governments, political parties, and paramilitary organizations, the progress toward peace will require individuals to break through the barriers dividing Northern Ireland's population. Current events and events dating back centuries shape the emotions and viewpoints of Northern Ireland's citizens. Many people have been directly affected by the con-

flict. Their family members or friends have been killed, injured, or put in prison. The people are angry and confused. In parts of Northern Ireland, many are unemployed and see little hope of finding a decent job in the future. Some who have good jobs worry that changes imposed by the government will hurt their standard of living. Fear of physical violence and fear of being unable to make a living have led

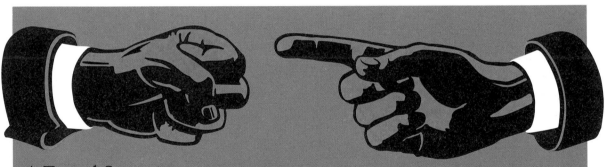

A Typical Scenario

When the paramilitary groups and the two governments hold tightly to their basic positions, attempts at peacemaking bog down. Their interactions typically go something like this: Catholic and Protestant paramilitary groups, who would have to stop their violent activities for peace to occur, show no interest in talking to one another. The PIRA will talk to the British but only to set the terms of the British withdrawal. The British officially refuse to talk to the PIRA unless a permanent cease-fire is declared. The PIRA views this condition as a request for surrender before they even get to the talks. Any step Britain takes to calm the PIRA, especially any offer to share power over the province with the Republic, strikes the militant loyalists as the beginning of the British abandonment they have always feared. The Protestant parties generally protest such moves, which they view as Britain giving in to terrorists, and become uncooperative. Only when this typical scenario is overcome can the difficult progress toward peace in Northern Ireland begin.

many people in the province to view people of the other religion as the source of the problems.

One challenge that faces the peace movement is to prevent people's negative feelings from leading them to participate in the violence. Paramilitary groups continue to recruit members who are discontent with Northern Ireland's society and who feel that violence is the only way to change the situation. Some people have grown up in militant nationalist or loyalist areas, where being involved with the paramilitary is respected and expected. Others who never thought about joining a paramilitary group feel differently after someone they know has been killed or they have experienced discrimination. Desire for retaliation has pushed some people to join paramilitary organizations.

But within Northern Ireland and abroad, many individuals and groups are working to counter the paramilitary actions that keep the violence going. Included in the effort are a small number of former paramilitary members who have realized that violence has not solved Northern Ireland's problems. After getting out of prison, some individuals have given up terrorism and become involved in community work to prevent young people from joining extremist groups. A former member of a Protestant paramilitary group said when he brings together Catholic and Protestant kids for outings they learn that "the other doesn't have a tail or three heads."

One peace-seeking group that works to bridge religious

"Growing up, I got to 17, and I was coming home past the Short Strand, and a gunman fired shots and I got shot in the shoulder. . . . This made me very angry, I was just walking down the street, no more. After that I got involved with one of the paramilitaries."

and political differences in Northern Ireland is the Corrymeela Community, a Christian organization founded in 1965. Their goal has been to create a safe place where people from different backgrounds can come together, talk, and begin to understand one another. Corrymeela runs a camp on the northern coast in Ballycastle and organizes groups throughout Northern Ireland. Each week of the summer, a group of people of every economic class, religion, and age live together at the camp, worship together, attend classes and workshops, and enjoy the feeling of safety that's often missing at home.

Corrymeela organizes programs for families or individuals and has special programs for teenagers. Because Corrymeela understands the importance of serving the whole society, it does not charge people who couldn't otherwise afford to attend the camp. Some Catholics and Protestants who come to Corrymeela have never spent time with anyone from the other religion. The rule governing Corrymeela is that everyone is accepted for who they are and for the views they hold. Those who run

Corrymeela hope that people who attend the camp or local meetings will learn that most people in Northern Ireland want peace and are not to be feared. When people

the presence of troops, and the restriction of personal rights are not the norm.

Peggy Barrett of Manheim, Pennsylvania, former president of the Children's

Friendship Project of Northern Ireland (CFPNI), emphasizes that the six-week stay in the United States is considered a "learning experience," not a vacation, for the teens they sponsor. Unlike most summer programs that place one child in an American household, CFPNI pairs a Catholic and a Protestant teen in the host family's home, where they share a room. The program matches teens of the same gender by

> *"Keith Browne from Larne is really friendly and funny. What a surprise when I find out he's Protestant. I wonder what my friends at home will think when I tell them I met a Protestant and he was really all right."*

are willing to interact with those outside of their own religion—and bring this willingness into their local communities—strong relationships can be formed between the Catholic and Protestant majorities who want peace. When strong relationships bridge the religions, violence conducted by extremist groups within each faction will no longer be able to divide the whole society.

A number of programs provides young children and teens with the opportunity to come to the United States and live with a host family for several weeks during the summer. These kids get the chance to see what life is like in a society where violence,

Children's Friendship Project of Northern Ireland, Inc.

Catholic and Protestant teenagers who had participated in the 1996 Children's Friendship Project of Northern Ireland got together for a reunion later that year.

their interests and by their homes' geographical proximity. Teens must live near enough to one another so they and their families can get together before and after the summer trip.

Because of segregation in Northern Ireland, many of these teens don't associate with people who are not of their own religion. In close quarters in a different society—far away from the prejudices in Northern Ireland—the two almost always find they have much in common. Barrett says some of the pairs have gone back to Northern Ireland and formed a group of friends that include teens from both religions. Some have become roommates in college, and some of their families vacation together.

Although the cease-fire ended in 1996, Barrett remains hopeful for Northern Ireland's future. Many teens, who experienced extended peace in Northern Ireland for the first time in their lives in 1994–1996, expressed a determination to create a lasting peace. According to Barrett, they say, "we will not raise our own children in the environment we've been raised in."

Younger Protestants and Catholics arrive in the United States to take part in another summer program called Project Children. It brings one child into an American home that has a child of roughly the same age. During the six weeks, the children enjoy simple pastimes far from the conflict.

Many other grassroots efforts at bringing peace to Northern Ireland are taken up by individuals. For example, after the PIRA bombing put an end to the 17-month cease-fire in February 1996, Gavin and Margaret Walker, a couple from Bangor (12 miles outside of Belfast), organized the campaign for No More Violence. The Walkers'

Jim Simondet

desire for their young son to grow up in a land without violence prompted them to take an active part in the peacemaking process. Through radio and television announcements, the Walkers asked people to write "No More Violence" on postcards and to send them immediately. Within five days, more than 500,000 cards and letters containing 750,000 signatures flooded in from throughout Northern Ireland, the Republic, and across Europe. People from every religion, age group, and socioeconomic level responded. One week after the bombing, the Walkers delivered bundles of the cards

After the cease-fire ended in 1996, Gavin and Margaret Walker urged citizens of all stripes to print "No More Violence" on postcards that would be collected and delivered to government officials. Three-quarters of a million people participated in sending this unique, nonviolent message.

to government officials in Northern Ireland, the Republic, and Britain.

PEACEMAKING RISKS

Being part of the peacemaking process at any level can be dangerous. John Hume, the leader of the SDLP, is praised for his efforts to bring about a political solution to the violence and to improve the economic conditions of the province. But the other side to his success is that over the years, hostile opponents have made threatening phone calls, sent hate mail, set his office on fire, vandalized his home, and attempted to kidnap his daughter. By trying to build a society that treats all citizens equally, Hume makes himself a target for nationalist and loyalist extremists.

Risks also exist for those who bridge segregation by simply having a friend who is not of the same religion. Paramilitary groups consider this "antisocial" behavior and have punished children as young as 10 years old. After a close friend was killed by a PIRA bomb, Marty Hannigan—a Protestant from Belfast—decided to organize meetings between Catholic and Protestant teens, hoping that communication would lead to understanding. The UDA, a Protestant paramilitary group, found out about the meetings and broke both his knees. This did not stop Marty's efforts: "I kept meeting with Catholics at the center. I wasn't going to let the UDA get away with it."

Duncan Morrow—who works with the Corrymeela Community and teaches politics at the University of Ulster in Jordanstown—considers the alternative, which is to remain segregated out of fear: " . . . if there is a lesson . . . in Northern Ireland it is that retreat into 'our own' is not safety. . . . Fear makes us defensive, makes us justify the unjustifiable, makes us indifferent to the sufferings of others, and makes us inhuman to each other." While a small proportion of Northern Ireland's population persists in its attempts to achieve political goals through violence, others—despite great personal risks—continue the search for peace.

Although they are rare, schools with integrated Catholic and Protestant student bodies exist. These girls go to an integrated school in Belfast.

© Ed Kashi

EPILOGUE*

Hopes rose among Northern Ireland's nationalists after the British election on May 1, 1997. The Labour Party won the majority of parliamentary seats, bringing to power Labour leader Tony Blair. During a visit to the province, Blair promised Northern Ireland's citizens he would work toward an overall settlement. In late May, British advisers met with Sinn Féin for the first time since the PIRA broke its cease-fire in February 1996. But Sinn Féin's leaders were unwilling to make commitments. Soon after the British-Sinn Féin meeting, peace talks—led by former U.S. senator George Mitchell—reopened without Sinn Féin and without a PIRA cease-fire.

The peace talks concluded in April 1998 with the Good Friday Agreement. Under its terms, Sinn Féin accepts that Northern Ireland will remain part of the United Kingdom, as long as a majority of the population is in favor. Power will devolve from Parliament in London to a new assembly and a Northern Ireland executive, which will be structured to ensure cross-community participation. There will be "North-South" bodies—linking northern and southern Ireland—and a British-Irish council, linking Ireland with Britain. Citizens in Northern Ireland and in the Irish republic have approved the agreement.

Endless haggling over decommissioning threatened the peace deal throughout 1999. But the Unionists eventually dropped their demand that decommissioning must precede Sinn Féin's entry into government. After 10 weeks of painstaking negotiations between the pro-agreement parties in Northern Ireland, Senator Mitchell returned to the United States, concluding that the basis existed for devolution to occur and for the formation of an executive to take place.

The province's new coalition government includes a former PIRA commander as minister for education and ministers from the DUP, which has consistently denounced the province's peace deal as a surrender to terrorism. The participants in Northern Ireland's new government have a long history of mutual hatred, but they have all agreed to work together to keep the peace agreement progressing.

*Please note: The information presented in *Northern Ireland: Troubled Land* was current at the time of the book's publication. For late-breaking news on the conflict, look for articles in the international section of U.S. daily newspapers. The *Economist,* a weekly magazine, is another good source for up-to-date information. You may also wish to access, via the Internet, the following newspapers: the *London Times* at http://www.the-times.co.uk/ and the *Belfast Telegraph* at http://www.belfasttelegraph.co.uk/.

CHRONOLOGY

A.D. 432   The missionary Patrick arrives in Ireland and begins to convert inhabitants to Catholicism.

1155   To bring Ireland into line with Catholic norms, Pope Adrian IV grants King Henry II of England lordship over the Irish.

1366   The English establish the Statutes of Kilkenny, which banned the use of Gaelic and forbade marriage between the Irish and the English.

1533   King Henry VIII establishes the Anglican Church. Most Irish remain loyal to Catholicism. Irish Catholics lose title to their land if they do not pledge loyalty to the king as head of the state and the new Anglican church.

1558   Queen Elizabeth I begins her reign, during which she outlawed Catholic religious services.

1607   Unwilling to live under English rule, substantial Ulster landowners flee to France. England imports loyal subjects to settle in northern Ireland, establishing a Protestant majority there.

1641   Catholics throughout the island rebel against Protestant oppression. They massacre many thousands of Protestants planted in Ulster.

1690   James II, the deposed Catholic English king, struggles to regain his crown from William of Orange in the Battle of the Boyne near Drogheda (July 1). William's Protestant troops win, and James II escapes to France.

1695   Although the English Parliament advocates treating Irish Catholics with more leniency, the all-Protestant Irish Parliament begins passing a series of anti-Catholic legislation known as the penal laws. The laws give second-class status to Irish culture.

1801   The legislatures of Great Britain and Ireland join together. The Act of Union created a new political unit called the United Kingdom of Great Britain and Ireland.

1829 The British Parliament passes the Roman Catholic Emancipation Act, which grants full legal equality to Catholics.

1845   The blight of Ireland's potato crop begins, wiping out several harvests and causing millions to starve and millions more to emigrate. The Irish viewed the aid Britain provided as insufficient.

1905   Nationalists in the south form Sinn Féin.

1914   The nationalists' long struggle to pass the Home Rule Bill, which would give the Irish a degree of self-government, succeeds but implementation is postponed because World War I (1914–1918) erupts.

1916   In Dublin, the Irish Republican Brotherhood leads a rebellion, known as the Easter Rising, against British rule. The British put down the revolt and kill the movement's leaders, which increases public support for Sinn Féin—at the time, the only legal political party that advocates an independent, united Ireland.

1919   Sinn Féin establishes the Dáil Éireann, a separate parliament in Dublin, and declares Irish independence. Britain attempts to reestablish control and to suppress the Dáil. The newly formed Irish Republican Army (IRA) responds with guerrilla warfare.

1920   The British propose the Government of Ireland Act, which would divide the island into two states, each still loosely connected with Great Britain. The act is accepted by the Protestant unionists in the north but creates disagreement between members of the Dáil.

1921   The Government of Ireland Act is ratified by six of the nine Ulster counties, and they officially become Northern Ireland, part of the United Kingdom of Great Britain and Northern Ireland. Some members of the Dáil support a proposal—the Anglo-Irish treaty—that the area outside of Protestant control becomes the Irish Free State, a self-governing dominion of the United Kingdom.

1922–1923 Civil War erupts between supporters of the Anglo-Irish treaty and opponents who want an independent, united Ireland. Treaty supporters win, and the Irish Free State is formed.

1937 The Irish Free State passes a new constitution and changes its name to Éire.

1949 In the Ireland Act, the British guarantee Northern Ireland's position as an integral part of the United Kingdom. Meanwhile, the Éirean government passes the Republic of Ireland Act 1948, which severs Éire's link with the United Kingdom and creates the Republic of Ireland.

1956–1962 The IRA conducts a terrorist campaign to drive the British from Northern Ireland.

1967 Activists form the Northern Ireland Civil Rights Association to organize nonviolent protests against inequality and anti-Catholic discrimination.

1968 Intercommunal riots occur. In October the Royal Ulster Constabulary (RUC) attack on Catholic marchers in Londonderry is filmed for international television.

1969 IRA membership splits. Those in favor of renewing violence form the Provisional Irish Republican Army (PIRA). Violence erupts in January as loyalist extremists attack civil rights marchers on the Burntollet Bridge while the RUC watches. Rioting spreads to nearby Londonderry. In August widespread rioting breaks out in Belfast and Londonderry. Britain sends army troops to take over security duties from Northern Ireland's Protestant-dominated forces.

1970–1971 The PIRA conducts a propaganda campaign to change Catholic opinion toward British security forces. British put antiterrorist measures, including internment, into place in August 1971.

1972 The number of fatalities due to the conflict peak in 1972. In January a demonstration, known as Bloody Sunday, results in the death of 13 unarmed civilians. Terrorist activities soar, causing the British to dismantle the Northern Ireland government and to impose direct rule in March.

1981 Hunger strike by Maze Prison inmates lowers international opinion of British rule.

1984 The PIRA bombs the annual Conservative Party conference in England. Prime Minister Margaret Thatcher narrowly escapes death.

1985 The governments of Britain and the Republic of Ireland present the Anglo-Irish Agreement, in which the British recognize as legitimate the Republic's interests in Northern Ireland. Unionists protest the consultative role offered to the Republic.

1993 The PIRA says it may halt acts of terrorism if Sinn Féin can participate in all-party talks. The government and Sinn Féin conduct secret meetings. Clandestine talks also take place between Social Democratic and Labour Party leader John Hume and Sinn Féin leader Gerry Adams. The Republic of Ireland agrees to put its claim of sovereignty over Northern Ireland to a vote before the Republic's population. In December Britain and the Republic issue the Downing Street Declaration.

1994 On August 31, the PIRA announces a cease-fire. Protestant paramilitaries join the cease-fire on October 13. The British government meets with Sinn Féin in December.

1995 Drawing protests from Northern Ireland unionists, Britain and the Republic endorse a "Framework for the Future" to coordinate policies on issues that affect the entire Irish island.

1996 On February 9, the PIRA breaks the cease-fire and sets off bombs in London. In Belfast peace talks that include all of Northern Ireland's political parties except Sinn Féin begin in June. In July the RUC decides not to allow the Orange Order to march through a Catholic area near Portadown, triggering five days of violent Protestant protests; when the RUC reverses its decision, Catholics begin two days of rioting. On October 7, the PIRA detonates two bombs within the British army's Northern Ireland headquarters in Lisburn, marking the first explosions in the province since 1994.

1997 On May 1, Labour leader Tony Blair is elected British prime minister. Peace talks resume in June without Sinn Féin. Violence escalates in June and July. On July 19, the PIRA announces that a cease-fire will begin on July 20, which may lead to Sinn Féin being admitted to talks in September. Loyalists' demands for PIRA disarmament may threaten progress of talks.

SELECTED BIBLIOGRAPHY

Bartlett, Jonathan, ed. *Northern Ireland*, Reference Shelf, vol. 54, no. 6. New York: H. W. Wilson, 1983.

Beirne, Barbara. *Siobhan's Journey: A Belfast Girl Visits the United States*. Minneapolis: Carolrhoda Books, 1993.

Bell, J. Bowyer. *The Irish Troubles: A Generation of Violence 1967–1992*. New York: St. Martin's Press, 1993.

Boyle, Kevin, and Tom Hadden. *Northern Ireland: The Choice*. New York: Penguin Books, 1994.

Chartres, John, Bert Henshaw, and Michael Dewer. *Northern Ireland Scrapbook*. London: Arms and Armour Press, 1986.

Flackes, W. D., and Sydney Elliott. *Northern Ireland: A Political Directory 1968–1993*. Belfast: Blackstaff Press, 1994.

Foster, R. F. *Modern Ireland 1600–1972*. New York: Viking Penguin, 1988.

Ireland in Pictures. Minneapolis: Lerner Publications, Geography Department, 1997.

Kronenwetter, Michael. *Northern Ireland*. New York: Franklin Watts, 1990.

Northern Ireland in Pictures. Minneapolis: Lerner Publications, Geography Department, 1997.

Parker, Tony. *May the Lord in His Mercy Be Kind to Belfast*. New York: Henry Holt, 1994.

Ranelagh, John O'Beirne. *A Short History of Ireland*. Cambridge: Cambridge University Press, 1983.

Taylor, Peter. *Families at War: Voices from the Troubles*. London: BBC Books, 1989.

INDEX

ABOUT THE AUTHOR

Eric Black, a journalist for the *Star Tribune* of Minneapolis-St. Paul, specializes in writing about the historical background of international situations. Black is the author of *Our Constitution: The Myth That Binds Us; Rethinking the Cold War;* and *Parallel Realities: A Jewish/Arab History of Israel/Palestine.* In 1979–1980, he was awarded an American Political Science Association Congressional Fellowship for a year of work and study in Washington, D.C. As recipient of the Knight Fellowship, he spent a year at Stanford University in 1985–1986. Black lives with his wife, Lauren Baker, and their two children, Rosie and Danny.

Eric Black/*Star Tribune* Photo

ABOUT THE CONSULTANT

Andrew Bell-Fialkoff, *World in Conflict* series consultant, is a specialist on nationalism, ethnicity, and ethnic conflict. He is the author of *Ethnic Cleansing,* published by St. Martin's Press in 1996, and has written numerous articles for *Foreign Affairs* and other journals. He is currently writing a book on the role of migration in the history of the Eurasian Steppe. Bell-Fialkoff lives in Bradford, Massachusetts.

SOURCES OF QUOTED MATERIAL

p.14 Tony Parker, *May the Lord in His Mercy Be Kind to Belfast* (New York: Henry Holt, 1994), 336; p.17 Steven Schroeder, "Toward a Higher Identity: An Interview with Mairead Corrigan Maguire," *Christian Century* 111, no. 13 (April 1994): 415; p. 18 Tony Parker, *May the Lord in His Mercy Be Kind to Belfast* (New York: Henry Holt, 1994), 145; p. 24 Robert Hirschfield, "Two Lads from Belfast Pursue Peace," *Christian Century* 107, no. 6 (Feb. 1990): 174; p.27 Seamus Heaney, "Belfast," in *Preoccupations: Selected Prose 1968–1978* (New York: Farrar, Straus, Giroux, 1980), 30; p. 59 Interview with Bernadette Devlin, *Playboy Magazine* 19 (Sept. 1972): 57; p. 59 Laurie Udesky, "Bernadette Devlin," *The Progressive* 54, no.7 (July 1990): 34; p. 64 Peter Taylor, *Families at War: Voices from the Troubles* (London: BBC Books, 1989), 111; pp. 68–69 William V. Shannon, "The Anglo-Irish Agreement," *Foreign Affairs* 64, no. 4 (Spring 1986): 851; p. 73 Associated Press, "9-Year-Old's Peace Wish Tugs at President, Crowd," *Minneapolis Star Tribune,* 1 Dec. 1995, 7A; p. 74 Kevin Cullen, "Blast Rocks London District; 36 Are Injured As Group Says IRA Truce Over," *Boston Globe,* 10 Feb. 96, 1; p. 74 *Washington Post,* "Major Shows Flexibility in His Tough Talk," *Minneapolis Star Tribune,* 13 Feb. 1996, 7A; p. 79 Margo Grimm, United Press International, 26 July 1983; p. 81 Robin Knight, "Uneasy Partners in an Infant Peace," *U.S. News and World Report,* 26 Dec. 1994, 92; p. 83 David Sharrock, "Blair Takes New Hope to Ireland," *Manchester Guardian Weekly* 156, no. 21 (25 May 1997): 1; p. 85 John Darnton, "Echoing in the Streets of Belfast, The Most Unexpected of Songs," *New York Times,* 21 July 1996, E7; p. 85 Ibid.; p. 86 Barbara Beirne, *Siobhan's Journey: A Belfast Girl Visits the United States* (Minneapolis: Carolrhoda Books, 1993), 33; p. 89 Robert Hirschfield, "Two Lads from Belfast Pursue Peace," *Christian Century* 107, no. 6 (Feb. 1990): 174; p. 89 Duncan Morrow, "Beyond Canary Wharf," *Corrymeela News,* Spring 1996, 3.